Engaging Method for Teaching Solfège

Shelley Tomich

Copyright © 2015 Shelley Tomich

ISBN-10: 0996085203

ISBN-13: 978-0-9960852-0-5

All rights reserved. Unless otherwise noted, images in this book are created by author or used with permission. No part of this publication, including images, may be reproduced, stored in a retrieval system, or transmitted in any form or by any means, electronic, mechanical, recording or otherwise, without the prior written permission of the author.

"Pitch Hill" is a registered trademark of Shelley Tomich.

Published by Pitch Publications

Printed in the United States of America

CONTENTS

	Preface	i
1	Solfège	1
2	Overview of Pitch Hill	3
3	Teaching Pitch, Lines, and Spaces	5
4	Scaredy-Cat Sol and Flat Head Mi	6
5	Hungry La	10
6	Boxer Do	12
7	Rooftop Re	14
8	Grumpy Fa	16
9	Mister Ti and Super Do (SD)	18
10	Pitch Hill Expanded	22
11	Lessons Using Pitch Hill	23
	Mi Sol: Here We Sit	24
	Mi Sol: Star Light, Star Bright	25
	Mi Sol La: Lucy Locket	26
	Mi Sol La: The Cow Who Clucked	27
	Mi Sol La: It's Raining, It's Pouring	28
	Do Mi Sol La: Apple Tree	30
	Do Re Mi: Hiccup Buttercup	32
	Do Re Mi: Froggy Learns to Swim	33
	Do Re Mi: Ten Little Fish	34

Do Re Mi Sol La: Round and Round	37
Do Re Mi Sol La: Mañana Iguana	38
Do Re Mi Sol La: Rainbow Fish	40
Do Re Mi Sol La: I Have a Car	42
Do Re Mi Fa Sol La: Silly Sally	44
Do Re Mi Fa Sol La: Over in the Meadow	45
Low-Sol Do Re Mi Fa Sol La: Fish and Chips and Vinegar	47
Low-Sol Do Re Mi Fa Sol La: Frère Jacques	49
Low-Sol Low-La Do Re Mi Fa Sol La: The Very Lazy Ladybug	51
Do Re Mi Fa Sol La Ti SD: Do-Do Bird	52
Do Re Mi Fa Sol La Ti SD: Pick a Pumpkin	53
Appendix A: Rubrics and Fun Sheets	55
Acknowledgements	76
About the Author	77

Preface

My original career goal was to be a middle school band director; I grew up in the band program and obtained my undergraduate degree in instrumental music. However, life has a way of taking unexpected turns, and I ended up teaching elementary music and chorus. I had to rely on many friends and mentors to find my way in this new career path.

One obstacle I faced as a teacher without a strong vocal background was teaching children to sing using solfège notes. I tried teaching solfège using traditional methods, but it bored my students (I was pretty miserable, too). They had no frame of reference for these "weird words" that are supposed to represent musical pitches.

At a local workshop I attended, the presenter discussed the power of literature in the classroom - the power of a story. I was inspired to write a story using the solfège syllables, and wrote the first draft of *Pitch Hill* on the back of the handouts for this program.

I shared this story with several friends; when others requested it, I decided I needed to write it down. The book is straightforward; I hope you and your students will find the simple story as much fun as my students have! *Pitch Hill* is based on the philosophy that children learn best when they are engaged in the material.

1. Solfège

Solfège syllables are the commonly preferred method of teaching singing; they work pure vowel sounds, aid in intonation, and allow a concrete method of rationalizing sound. In music classes growing up, I thought the term "solfège" was "soul fish," because of the way my music teacher pronounced it. I never understood what music had to do with an aquarium! I was in high school by the time I understood solfège was a term for the notes of the musical scale and "When you know the notes to sing, you can sing most anything!" (Line from "Do Re Mi" – Rogers and Hammerstein's *The Sound of Music*).

In the eleventh century, an Italian monk named Guido of Arezzo developed a six-note scale based on the first verse of a Latin hymn; each new line of the poem starts a new scale degree. My students love reading about Guido of Arezzo using the book, *Do Re Mi: If You Can Read Music, Thank Guido D'Arezzo* by Susan Roth (ISBN: 0618465723).

Translation:

So that your servants may, with loosened voices, resound the wonders
of your deeds, clean the guilt from our stained lips, O Saint John.

In the 1600's "Ut" was changed to "Do," and "Si" was added to complete the steps of the scale. Sarah Glover later changed "Si" to "Ti" so that every syllable begins with a different letter. In the 1800's, John Curwen created a series of hand-signs to accompany each syllable; these signs are still used today in music classes, notably as part of the Kodály method of teaching.

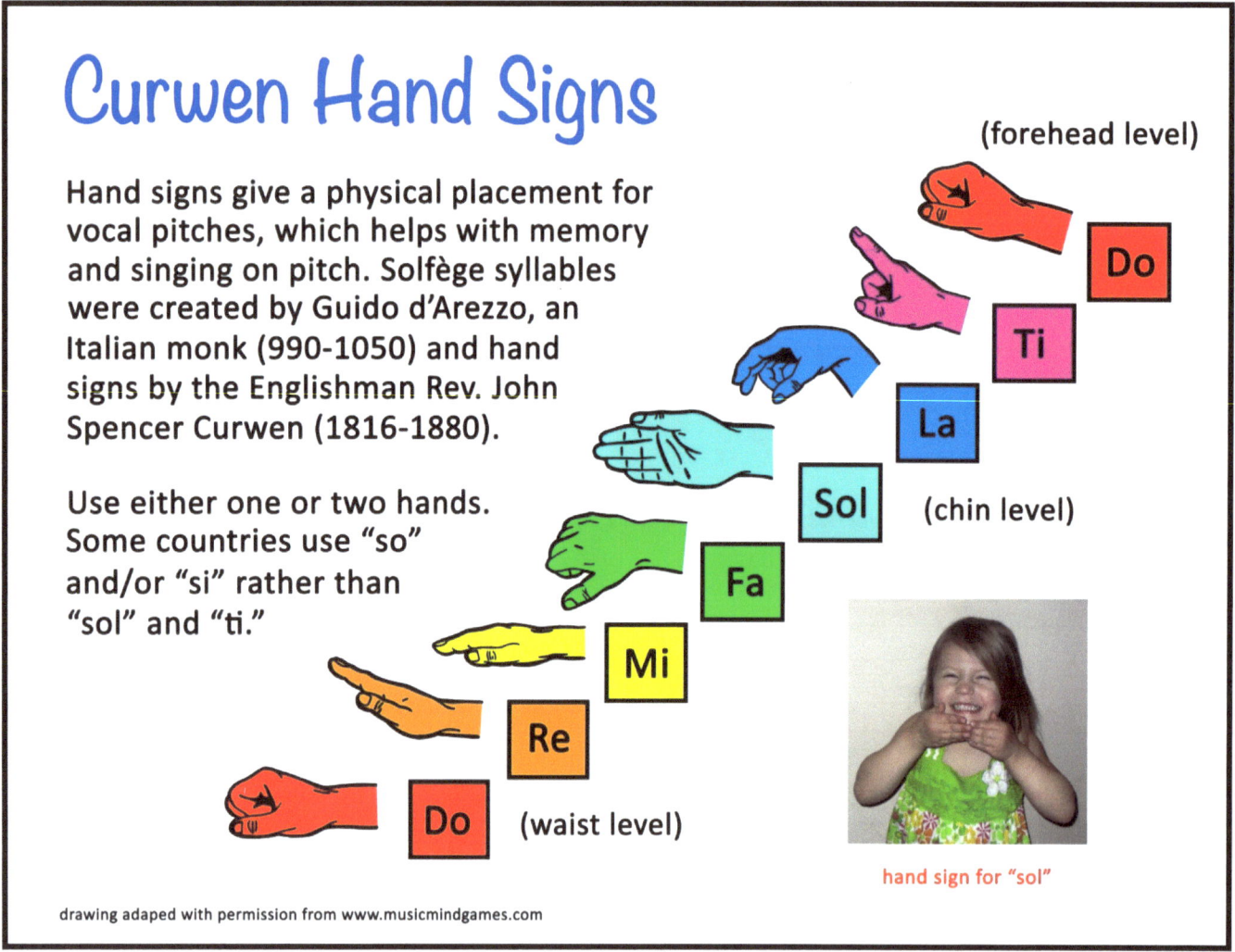

Pitch Hill is designed to visually represent solfège sounds, as well as captivate students in wonderful storytelling. The stories engage auditory, visual, and kinesthetic learners in one combined method. I hope you enjoy your visit to *Pitch Hill;* your students will become better musicians during your travels.

2. Overview of Pitch Hill

Welcome to *Pitch Hill! Pitch Hill* is a giant hill with the five lines and four spaces running through it; the Solfège People live on these lines and spaces. Characters who live lower on the hill have a lower pitch than those that live higher on the hill. There are four boys on *Pitch Hill* (Do/Super Do, Mi, Sol, and Ti) and three girls (Re, Fa, and La). When I introduce the characters to students I do so in this order: Lines and Spaces, Sol and Mi, La, Do, Re, Fa, Ti and Super Do (referred to as "SD").

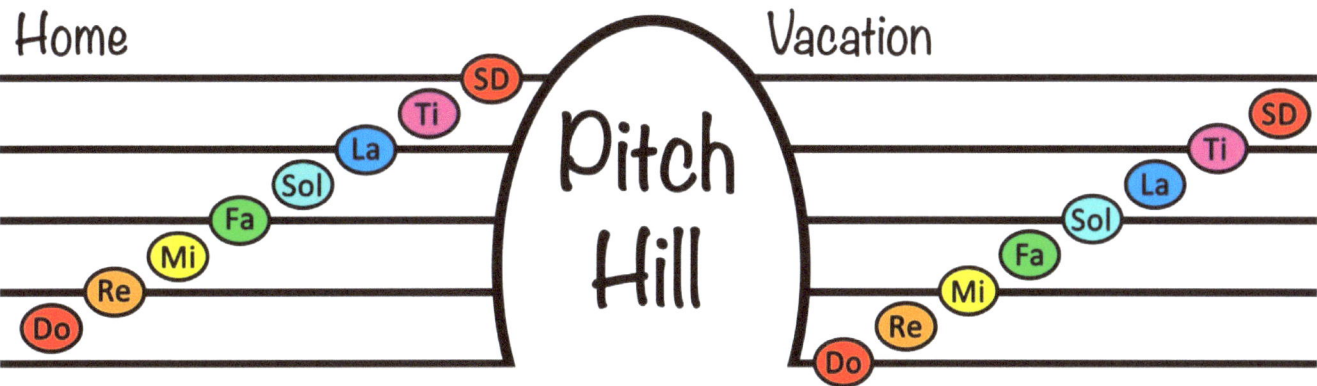

On the left side of the hill, the Solfège People have their "regular home"; on the right side they have their "vacation home." The Solfège People don't get to travel very far to neat places like Disney World®, the beach, or the mountains; they only go to other side of *Pitch Hill!* At home, the boys live in spaces and the girls live on lines; on vacation, they switch! This method familiarizes students to the concept of a moveable-do system.

In the beginning, I place Do in the bottom space/line; after students are familiar with the story, I move him to other various spots, shifting the other characters correspondingly. If the notes move onto ledger lines, I explain towns can create new neighborhoods, extending the boundaries of their town.

With the introduction of each character, I have my students complete a fun sheet (worksheet), sing songs, play instruments, participate in games, and do activities on the interactive white board. I have included a few of these songs and fun sheets for you. Though the use of technology enhances the story, I have also taught the story using only a simple chalkboard; the kids still loved it!

Each character in the *Pitch Hill* story is a different color. The colors correlate the seven steps of the musical scale with the seven colors of the rainbow: Red - Do, Orange - Re, Yellow - Mi, Green - Fa, Turquoise - Sol, Indigo Blue - La, and Violet - Ti (Remember Roy G. Biv?). Isaac Newton theorized pitches would be seen as the corresponding color of the rainbow if one could actually hear a specific color. I also find this correlation convenient when working with color-coded instruments such as Boomwhackers® and 8-Note Handbells.

3. Teaching Pitch, Lines, and Spaces

I begin the lesson on pitch with the book, *Buzz and Ollie's High, Low Adventure* by Donna Sloan Thorne and Marilyn Sloan Felts (ISBN: 0972414703). After reading the book, students explore high and low sounds in the classroom and in their life. We also sing, play, and move to high and low sounds.

Next, I draw the hill part of *Pitch Hill,* and we discuss the picture as a class (giant hill, go up and down, etc.) Then I draw the word "Pitch" in the middle. Students really understand this concept when we compare how the word pitch is used in baseball and music – when one pitches a baseball, it goes up and then comes down.

Draw lines going through *Pitch Hill* and talk about line and space notes. Have students identify these notes, practice drawing them, and identify them as high and low. I have a giant music staff rug that we also throw beanbags on, but I have thrown them onto poster board lines and masking tape lines in situations with fewer resources. I am also thankful to have an interactive white board in my room; I have several interactive slides students can use to identify lines and spaces. Finally, students complete a fun sheet identifying lines and spaces (see Appendix A).

4. Scaredy-Cat Sol and Flat Head Mi

Sol and mi are often the first pitches taught in elementary classrooms; there are many available two-note songs using sol and mi. Isolating these patterns minimizes vocal and hand movement, and familiarizes students with the concept that pitches have spatial relationships on the music staff.

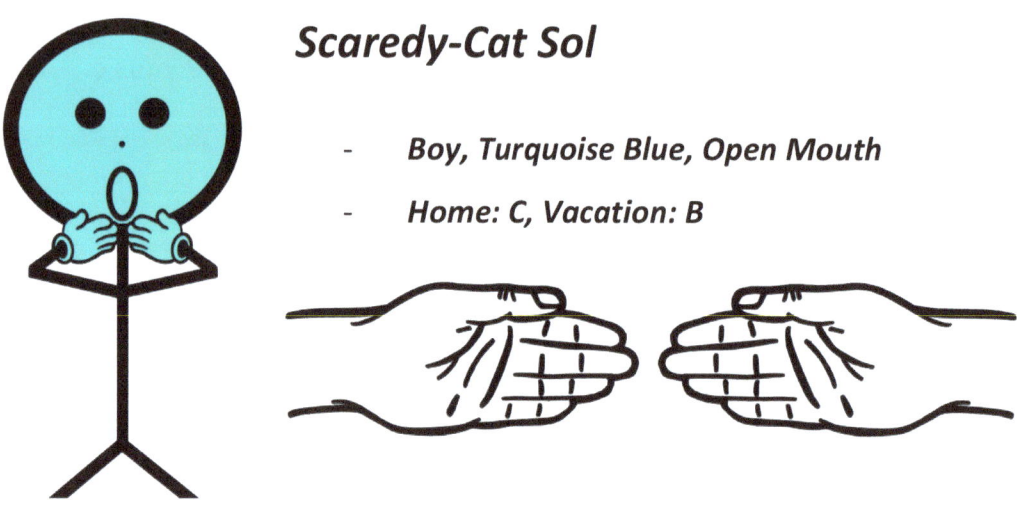

Scaredy-Cat Sol

- *Boy, Turquoise Blue, Open Mouth*
- *Home: C, Vacation: B*

Explain to students:

Sol is the first character; he is a turquoise blue boy with an open mouth as if surprised. Sol looks this way because he is a scaredy-cat; he is afraid of *everything!* When he leaves his house, you can see him visibly shaking and peeking around corners and out doors. When he finally emerges, he is just barely peeking out from behind his eyes, terrified that something will surprise him! Therefore he keeps his hands in front of his face, just peeking out! We call him "Scaredy-Cat Sol"

Sing the "Sol Song" with students:

Sol Song

Shelley Tomich

Teach students about Sol's home on Pitch Hill:

Sol lives in the third space at home, but when he goes on vacation, he doesn't go very far; he just goes to the other side of *Pitch Hill!* When he goes to the other side of *Pitch Hill*, he does something very, very tricky – he moves from a space to a line!

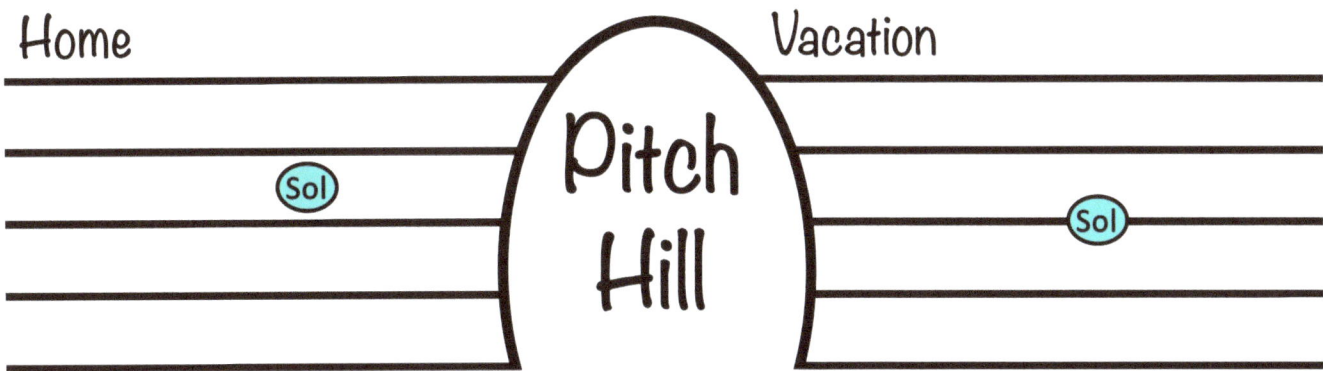

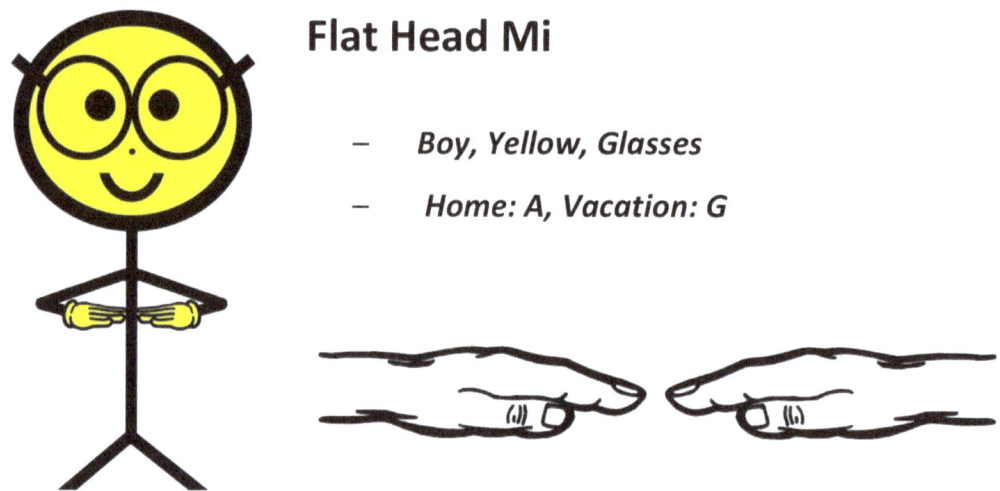

Flat Head Mi

- *Boy, Yellow, Glasses*
- *Home: A, Vacation: G*

Explain to students:

Mi is the second character introduced in *Pitch Hill*. When teaching Mi, I make a point to show the spelling of Mi and how it isn't *me,* Mrs. Tomich, but *Mi*, the music note! Mi has *extremely* large glasses. Like many of us, he doesn't have perfect eyesight. However, when his mom took him to the eye doctor to get new glasses, they were all out of fashion glasses (I usually point out the "cool, sophisticated" glasses found on students around the room).

Poor Mi had to get giant glasses! He absolutely hates them! They are unattractive, and they keep falling off his face; when they fall off his face, he can't see anything! Mi tries to convince people he's fine without his glasses, but he keeps running into the walls so much that his head has flattened out! Therefore, his hand sign is flat hands and we call him "Flat-head Mi."

Sing the "Mi Song" with students:

Mi Song

Shelley Tomich

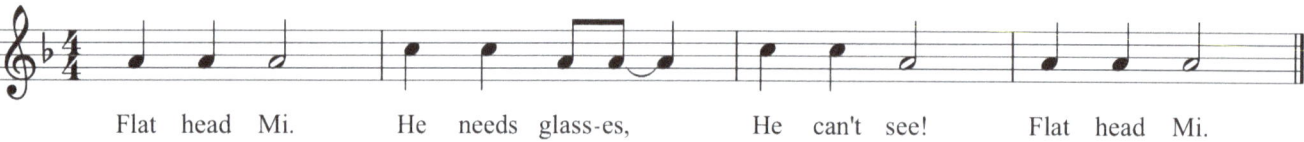

Teach students about Mi's home on Pitch Hill:

Mi is a lower note than Sol. On *Pitch Hill,* he lives in the space below Sol at home, and on vacation he lives on the line below Sol! To take the concept a step further, explain Sol and Mi are buddies and really like to hang out together. This helps build the foundation of pitches that follow one another in a song and/or builds the first step in constructing basic chords.

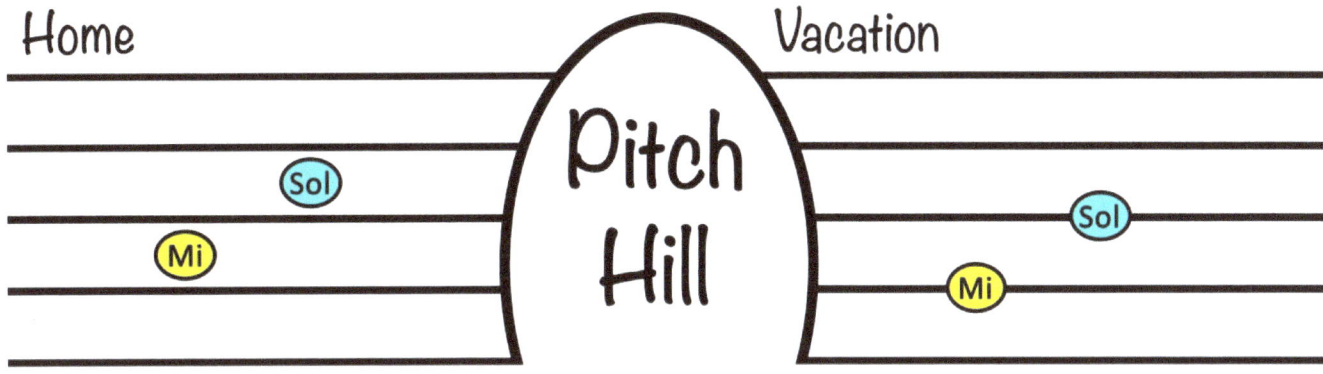

Suggested Songs to Practice Mi and Sol:

- "Bee, Bee, Bumblebee" – American Game Song
- "Bye, Bye, Baby-O" – American song
- "Charlie Over the Water" – Folk song from the United States
- "Cuckoo, Cuckoo" – Words and music by Aden G. Lewis
- "Engine, Engine, Number Nine" – Folk song from the United States
- "Hey, Hey, Look at Me" – Traditional playground song
- "Here We Sit" – Game song from the United States
- "In and Out" – American song
- "Lemonade" – Game song from the United States
- "One, Two, Buckle My Shoe" – English folk song
- "Quaker, Quaker" – American song
- "See-saw" – American song
- "Serra, Serra, Serrador" – Folk song from Brazil
- "Star Light, Star Bright" – Folk song from the United States
- "Tinker, Tailor" – English button counting song
- "Two, Four, Six, Eight" – English nursery rhyme

5. Hungry La

Hungry La

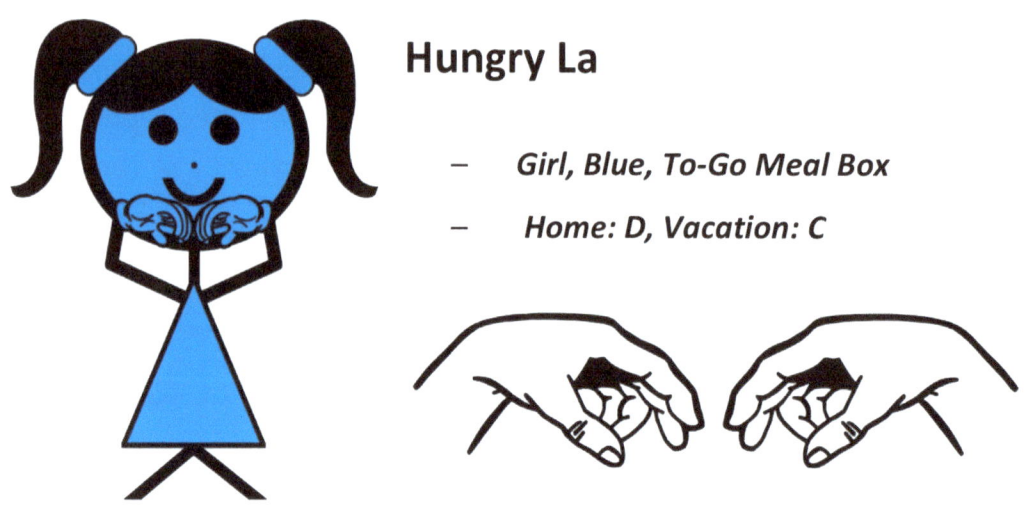

- *Girl, Blue, To-Go Meal Box*
- *Home: D, Vacation: C*

Explain to students:

La is our first lovely lady! However, she has a very sad story; her mom and dad are terrible, horrible, rotten, very bad cooks! They burn *everything!* Hamburgers, hot dogs, macaroni and cheese, potato chips – yes, even potato chips (don't ask how). Because it is so hard to find something eatable at home, La goes to the only restaurant in *Pitch Hill:* McDonalds! La enjoys ordering apple slices and a glass of milk with her hamburger! La's hand signs look like an "M" for McDonalds. (All the girls in my class look forward to the introduction of our first female character!)

Sing the "La Song" with students:

La Song

Shelley Tomich

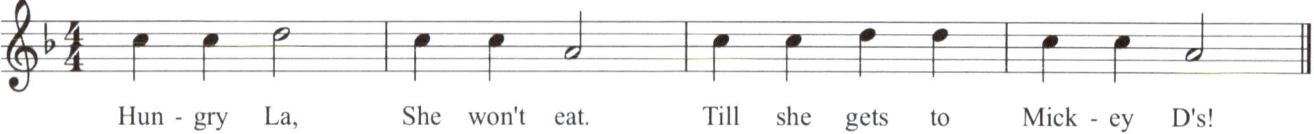

Teach students about La's home on Pitch Hill:

I remind students our boy characters, Sol and Mi, live in spaces at home and on lines on vacation. The girls have homes that are opposite of the boys; when the girls are in spaces, the boys are on lines and vice versa.

La is Sol's best friend! They love being very close; in fact, La lives right next door to Sol! La's house is on the line above Sol at home. When La goes on vacation, she switches to a space! I remind students not to put La right on top of Sol; you wouldn't want someone to build a house on top of your house! (You can go into harmony and chords another day). This helps provide a foundation for La and Sol commonly being found next to one another in songs.

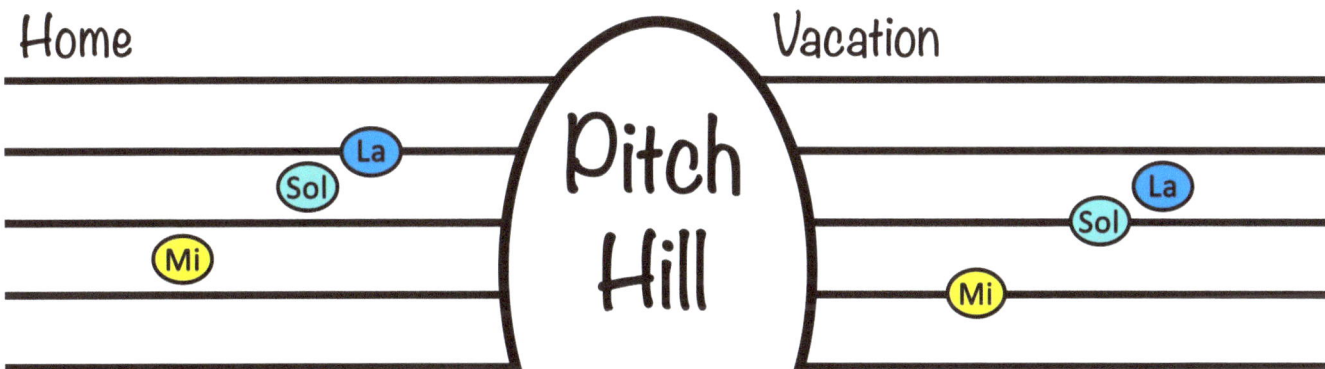

Suggested Songs to Practice Mi, Sol, and La:

- "Acka Backa" – Traditional game song from North America
- "Bounce High, Bounce Low" – Game song from the United States
- "Duerme, Mi Tesoro" – Folk song from Puerto Rico
- "It's Raining, It's Pouring" – Traditional song from the United States
- "Oliver Twist" – Traditional song of the British Isles and the United States
- "On a Log, Mister Frog" – Traditional Children's song of the United States
- "Pizza, Pizza, Daddy-O" – African American singing game
- "Rain, Rain, Go Away" – Traditional Children's song
- "Se, Se, Se" – Hand game song from Japan
- "Snail, Snail" – Traditional song from the United States
- "We Are Playing in the Forest" – American singing game

6. Boxer Do

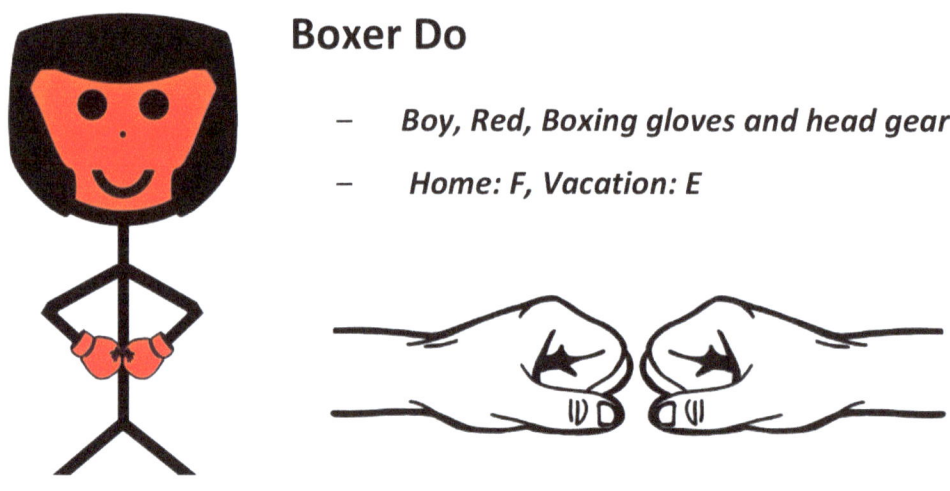

Boxer Do

- *Boy, Red, Boxing gloves and head gear*
- *Home: F, Vacation: E*

Explain to students:

Do is the lowest note found in *Pitch Hill*. Do wears a funny looking hat and funny looking gloves! This is the gear for his favorite sport – boxing! Boxing can be very dangerous so he wears this protective gear. His hand sign is the boxing gloves together in an "I'm tough" stance, and we call him "Boxer Do."

Sing the "Do Song" with students:

Do Song

Shelley Tomich

Box-er Do. He's so strong. All day long. Box-er Do!

Teach students about Do's home on Pitch Hill:

Do is the lowest note on *Pitch Hill* – he lives in the lowest space at home and the lowest line on vacation.

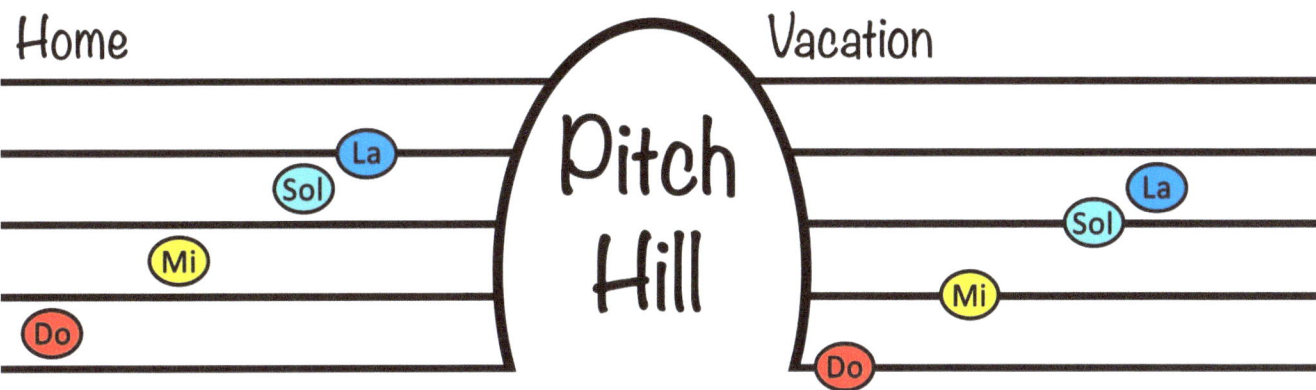

Suggested Songs to Practice Do, Mi, Sol, and/or La:

- "Andy Pandy" – Traditional song from the United States (d m s)
- "Apple Tree"- Traditional song from the United States
- "Donkey, Donkey" – Old English rhyme
- "Hunting Song" – Native American song (s, d m s l)
- "Little Sally Walker" – African American singing game
- "Mother, Mother" – Traditional (d m s)
- "Mr. Frog" – Traditional song from the United States
- "My Owlet" – Native American folk song
- "Ring Around the Rosy" – Traditional English game song
- "Sorida" – Game song from Shona people of Zimbabwe (d m s)
- "Trot Old Joe" – Texas folk song (s, l, d m)
- "Wee Willie Winkie" – Traditional nursery rhyme

7. Rooftop Re

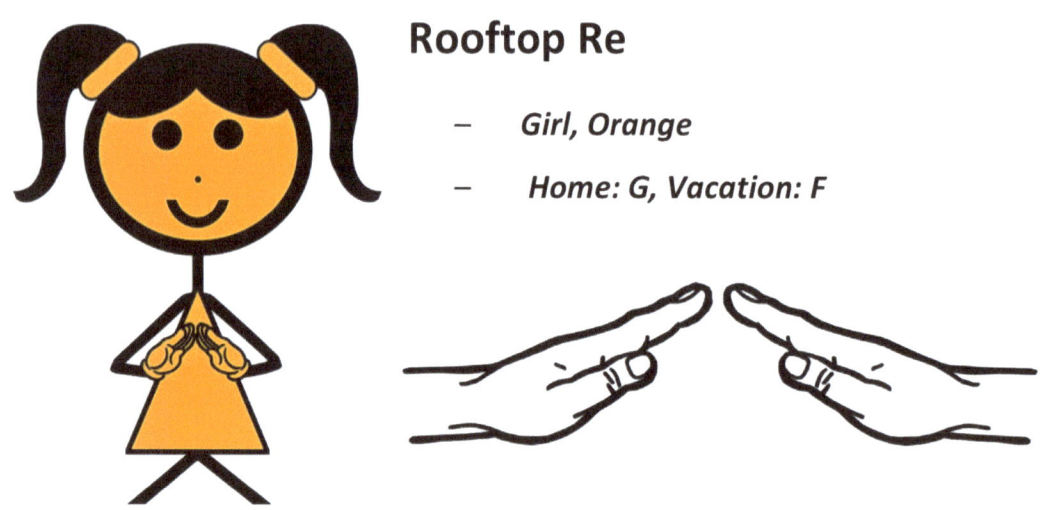

Rooftop Re

- *Girl, Orange*
- *Home: G, Vacation: F*

Explain to students:

Re is the second girl to join the *Pitch Hill* stories. Re is a future astronomer; she adores looking at the stars. Since she loves the stars so much, she does something children should *never, ever* do…she goes upstairs in her house, opens the window, and climbs out onto the roof! This is very dangerous, and one should never do this at home! Because she goes on the roof, we call her "Rooftop Re," and her hand sign is a small rooftop.

Sing the "Re Song" with students:

Re Song

Shelley Tomich

Teach students about Re's home on Pitch Hill:

Re is one of the lower notes and she lives between Do and Mi. I tell students that she lives above Do because if she fell off the roof, Do would catch her (he's really strong because of his boxing workouts). She lives by Mi because he couldn't tattle-tell on her for going on the roof (remember he can't see without his glasses). Re lives on a line at home and lives in a space on vacation.

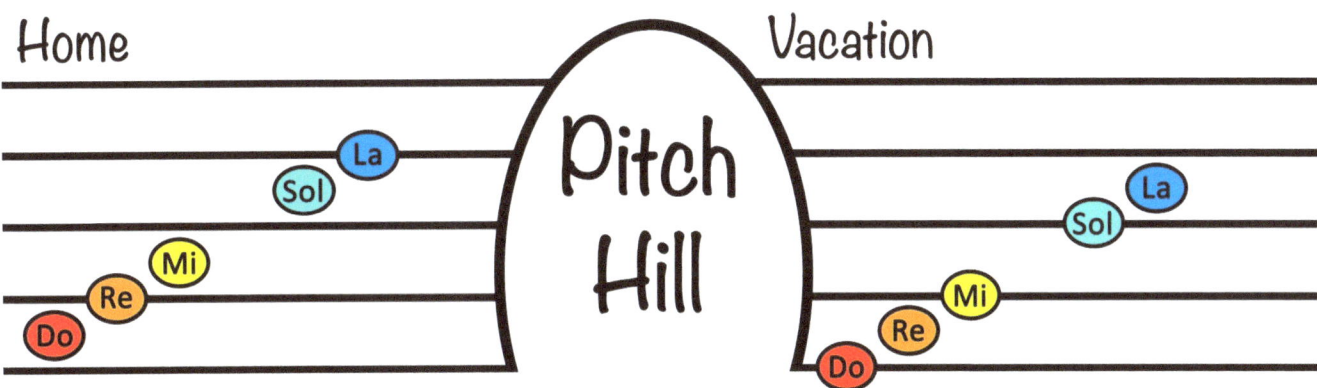

Suggested Songs to Practice Do, Re, Mi, Sol, and/or La:

- "All Around the Buttercup" – Traditional singing game from the United States
- "Button, You Must Wander" – American singing game
- "Bow, Wow, Wow!" – Mother Goose rhyme
- "Cookie" – Calypso song from the West Indies
- "Great Big House" – Play-party song from Louisiana
- "Here Comes a Bluebird" – American Singing Game
- "Ida Red" – Kentucky Folk Song
- "Rocky Mountain" – Folk song from the Southern United States
- "Sally Go Round the Sun" – Nursery rhyme
- "Teddy Bear" – American play song
- "Wake Me, Shake Me" – American folk song
- "Dinah" – Folk song from the United States (d r m s)
- "Alabama Gal" – Folk song from Alabama (s, l, d r m s)
- "All Night, All Day" – African American spiritual (s, l, d r m s)
- "Chicken on the Fence Post" – Play-party song from the United States (s, l, d r m s l)
- "Turn the Glasses Over" – Folk song from the United States (s, l, d r m s l)

8. Grumpy Fa

Grumpy Fa

- *Girl, Green, Frowning*
- *Home: B, Vacation: A*

Explain to students:

You might notice Fa is frowning. Fa is a very grumpy, sad person. Her mom *loves* the color green. She dresses her daughter in green, they have a green house, they eat green foods (broccoli, asparagus, veggie juice, etc.), and they have green furniture. Guess what color Fa hates? Green! Therefore she walks around with her thumbs down; she is known as "Grumpy Fa."

Sing the "Fa Song" with students:

Fa Song

Shelley Tomich

Grum-py Fa, She hates green! It's the worst col-or she's ev-er seen!

Teach students about Fa's home on Pitch Hill:

Fa lives between Mi and Sol; she wanted to be next to the people that were least likely to notice everything in her life is green. Mi can't see her and Sol is such a scaredy cat, he really is only concerned about things that could scare him! Since Fa is a girl, she will live on a line at home and in a space on vacation.

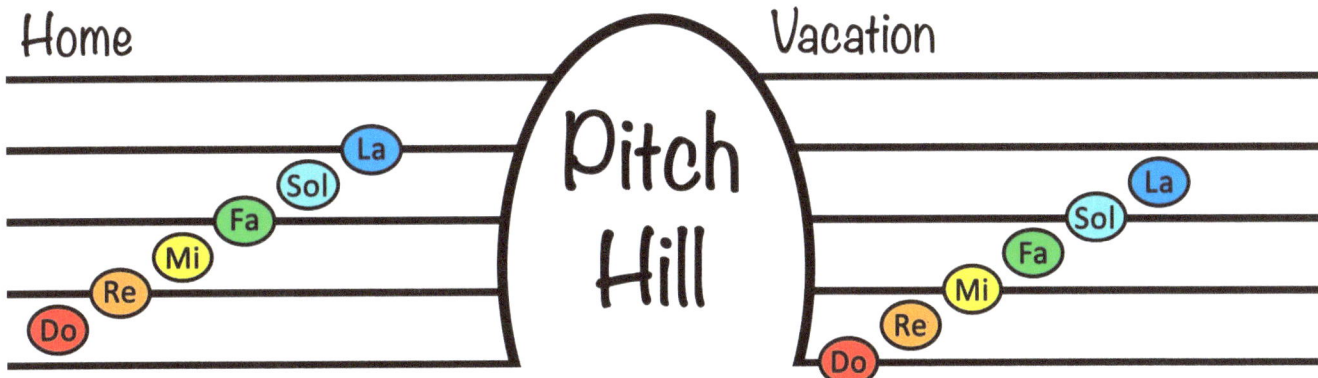

Suggested Songs to Practice Do, Re, Mi, Fa, Sol, and/or La:

- "A-Tisket, A-Tasket" – Folk song from the United States
- "Counting Song" – Children's song from Mexico
- "I Caught a Rabbit" – Kentucky folk song
- "I've a Pair of Fishes" – Yiddish folk song
- "Jim Along, Josie" – American folk song
- "Juba" – African American folk song (d r m f)
- "Kum Ba Yah" – Traditional African song
- "Lady, Lady" – Traditional lullaby from the United States (d r m f s)
- "Little Red Caboose" – Traditional children's song
- "London Bridge" – Game song from England
- "Michael, Row the Boat Ashore" – African American Spiritual
- "My Thumbs are Starting to Wiggle" - Traditional
- "Number One" – Counting and adding song
- "One Finger, One Thumb" - Traditional
- "Oh, A-Hunting We Will Go" – English folk song
- "Rock-A My Soul" – Spiritual
- "This Old Man" – English folk song
- "When the Saints Go Marching In" – American gospel hymn (d r m f s)

9. Mister Ti and Super Do (SD)

I often teach Ti and Super Do in the same lesson; in music the note Ti is often found with a Do nearby. In the *Pitch Hill* story, Ti and Super Do are best friends so teaching them together comes naturally in the lesson.

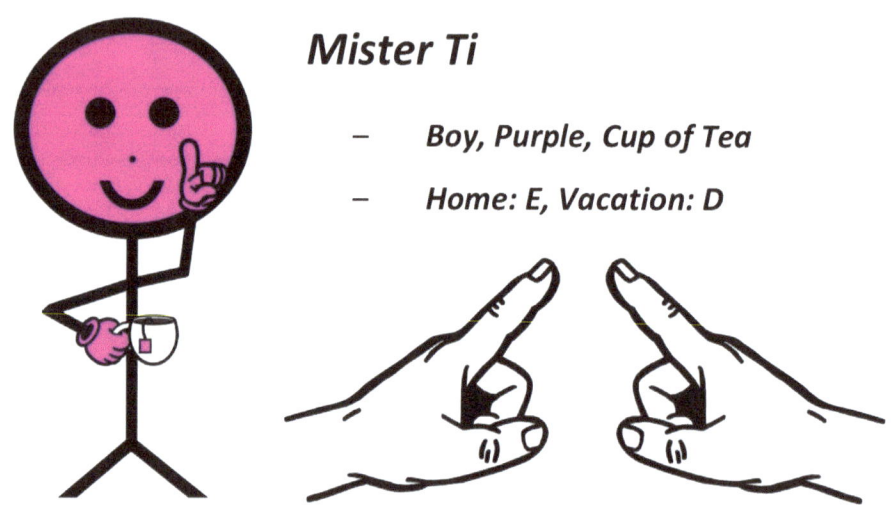

Mister Ti

- *Boy, Purple, Cup of Tea*
- *Home: E, Vacation: D*

Explain to students:

Ti is our exchange student; he grew up in England and participates in the English tradition of afternoon tea. His tea is served hot and in a small cup. He sips at it very delicately and often enjoys crumpets (a bread item similar to an English muffin). He invites his best friend, Do, over for tea, and orders one cup of tea for himself and one cup of tea for his friend (hold up the index finger with one finger on each hand). We politely call him "Mr. Ti."

Sing the "Ti Song" with students:

Ti Song

Shelley Tomich

Come with me! Have a cup of tea! Sip and eat with Mis-ter Ti!

Teach students about Ti's home on Pitch Hill:

Ti enjoys living in the north (high) part of *Pitch Hill* because it reminds him of his homeland. At home, he lives in the fourth space and on vacation he lives on the fourth line.

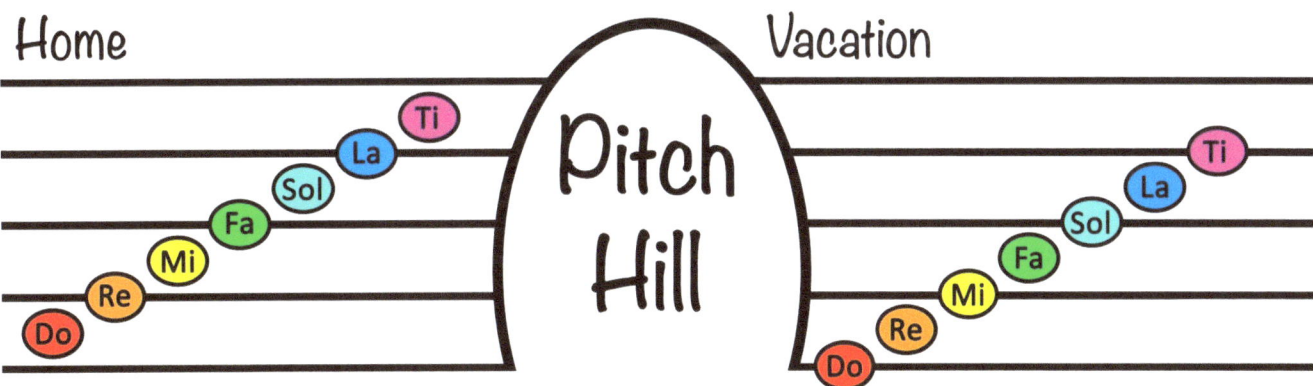

Super Do

- *Boy, Red, Cape and mask*
- *Home: F, Vacation: E*

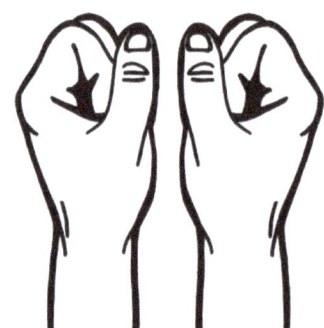

Explain to students:

Ti and Do are best friends; unfortunately, Ti and Do live very far apart! It would take a long time for Do to drive up to Ti's house. Therefore, Do puts on mask, puts on a cape, and becomes *Super Do!* Super Do is out to help the world create music (and drink tea with Ti). Super Do's hand sign is the fists high in the air like he is flying, and he is commonly referred to as "SD."

Sing the "SD Song" with students:

SD Song

Shelley Tomich

Teach students about SD's home on Pitch Hill:

When Do becomes Super Do, he goes way up high on *Pitch Hill* and does something really strange. You know how all the boys live in spaces at home and on lines on vacation? Well this changes when our characters become super heroes. Super Do goes from the lowest space to the highest line and on vacation, from the lowest line to the highest space! Don't let Super Do fool you!

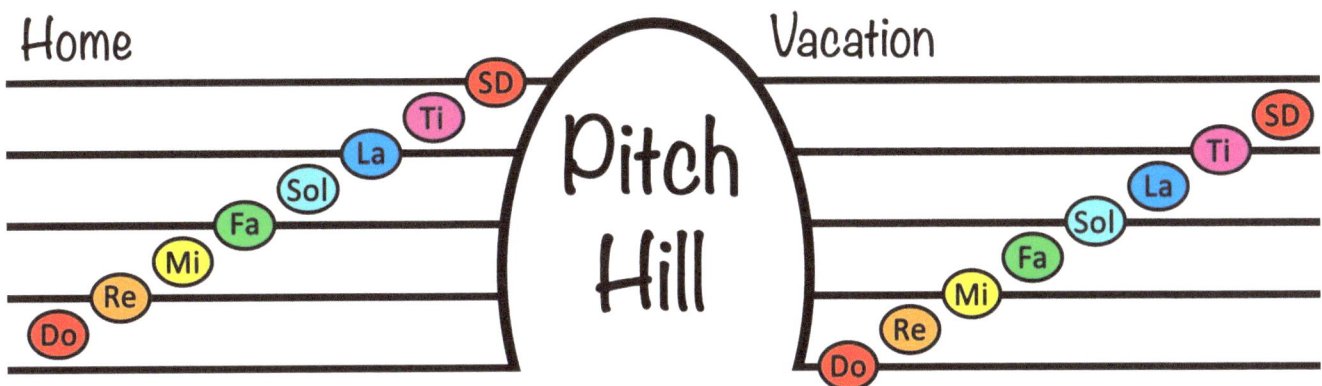

Suggested Songs to Practice Do, Re, Mi, Fa, Sol, La, Ti, and/or SD

- "Apples and Bananas" – Traditional game song from the United States (t, d r m f)
- "Children, Go Where I Send Thee" – African American spiritual (t, d r m f s d')
- "Day-O! (Banana Boat Loader's Song) – Folk song from Jamaica (s, t, d r m f s l t d')
- "Ding, Dong, Diggidong" – from Orff-Keetman, *Orff-Schulwerk, Vol. 1* (d r m s l d')
- "Don't Let the Wind" – Folk song from St. Helena Island (d r m s l d')
- "Down in the Meadow" – Folk song from the United States (m s l d')
- "El barquito" – Folk song from Latin America
- "El coqui" – Folk song from Puerto Rico
- "Grizzly Bear" – Traditional children's song (t, d r m f s)
- "John Jacob Jingleheimer Schmidt" – American camp song (s, l, t, d r m f s l)
- "Kye Kye Kule" – Call and Response Song from Ghana (d r m f s d')
- "Li'l Liza Jane" – folk song from the United States (d r m s l d')
- "Make New Friends" – Traditional Round (s, d r m f s d')
- "My Head and My Shoulders" – Zulu singing game
- "Over the River and Through the Wood" – American folk melody
- "Skip to My Lou" – Folk song from the United States (t, d r m f s)
- "Tideo" – Play-party song from Texas (d r m s l d')

10. Pitch Hill Expanded

Pitch Hill is intended to be a supplement to the activities you do in the classroom. As you get further in the stories, and the students get older and/or more capable, you will expand students' knowledge beyond the scope of this program.

When I need to teach Low Sol and Low La, I tell students that Sol and La stand on their heads! They get a kick out of the idea of them doing headstands. When I need to expand beyond Super Do, I have the other characters dress up as superheroes and join Super Do in his fight for good music!

By the time I get to the sharp/flat solfège, I am beyond the stories of *Pitch Hill*. When I need characters for this purpose, I tell students that a few of the characters have twin brothers or sisters! The twins look alike and live in the same house (same line/space), but sound different.

11: Lessons Using Pitch Hill

Each lesson should follow the story of the *Pitch Hill* characters used in the story. These lessons often take multiple class periods to complete depending on how many activities you choose to do with each lesson (fun sheets, games, instruments, performing assessments, etc.). For each lesson, I have provided National Music Standards (NS), National Core Arts Standards (NCAS), applicable inter-disciplinary connections, teaching procedure, and assessment tools. Additional materials to enhance *Pitch Hill* lessons such as posters and interactive white board files can be purchased at www.PitchHill.com.

Mi Sol: Here We Sit

Objectives (with National Standards and National Core Arts Standards)
- Sing, alone and with others, a varied repertoire of music. (NS 1; NCAS 5.1)
- Use a system (solfège) to read simple pitch notation on the staff. (NS 5; NCAS 4.2)

Teaching Procedures
1. Introduce/review with students Sol and Mi from *Pitch Hill.*
2. Teach traditional game song "Here We Sit" first on solfège, then with lyrics.
3. When students have learned song, have them play the game:
    a. Have students sing the song with their eyes closed. Have one student go hide somewhere in the room (behind a desk, in a closet, etc.). Have remaining students open eyes when the song is over and try to guess who is missing.
    b. To make the game go faster, add additional students each time (Sing "Two of us...Three of us....Four of us...." Until the whole class has a turn to hide.
    c. Variation: Choose two students to close their eyes and the rest of the class sings. When the song is over it is a race to see which student can figure out who is hiding and call the missing student's name out.
4. Practice identifying Sol and Mi notes on the music staff.
5. Instruct students to complete fun sheet on Sol and Mi (Appendix A).

Assessment Tools
- Singing rubric (Appendix A).
- Sol and Mi paper assessment (Appendix A).

Here We Sit

Traditional Game Song

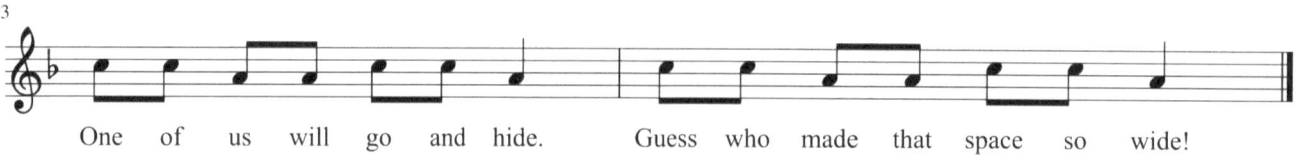

Mi Sol: Star Light Star Bright

Objectives (with National Standards and National Core Arts Standards)
- Sing, alone and with others, a varied repertoire of music. (NS 1; NCAS 5.1)
- Perform on instruments, alone and with others, a varied repertoire of music. (NS 2; NCAS 4.2; NCAS 5.1)
- Use a system (solfège) to read simple pitch notation on the staff. (NS 5; NCAS 4.2)
- Understand relationships between music and disciplines outside the arts. (NS 8; NCAS 11)

Inter-disciplinary Connections
- Science

Teaching Procedures
1. Introduce/review with students Sol and Mi from Pitch Hill.
2. Teach traditional folk song "Star Light Star Bright," first on solfège, then with lyrics.
3. Have students practice identifying Sol and Mi notes in song.
4. Have students sing a cappella and then with teacher adding accompaniment on bass xylophone.
5. Have students play xylophone on open C and F (take other bars off).
6. Instruct students to complete fun sheet on Sol and Mi (Appendix A).

Assessment Tools
- Singing rubric (Appendix A).
- Performing on Instruments rubric (Appendix A).
- Identifying Sol and Mi paper assessment (Appendix A).

Star Light Star Bright

Traditional Song

Star light, star bright, First star I see to-night.

Wish I may, wish I might, have the wish I wish to-night.

Mi Sol La: Lucy Locket

Objectives (with National Standards and National Core Arts Standards)
- Sing, alone and with others, a varied repertoire of music. (NS 1; NCAS 5.1)
- Sing in groups with appropriate dynamic levels. (NS 1; NCAS 5.1; NCAS 4.3)
- Use a system (solfège) to read simple pitch notation on the staff. (NS 5; NCAS 4.2)
- Use appropriate terminology in explaining music performances. (NS 6; NCAS 4.3; NCAS 8.1)

Teaching Procedures
1. Introduce/review with students Mi, Sol, and La from *Pitch Hill*.
2. Teach traditional game song "Lucy Locket" first on solfège, then with lyrics.
3. Play game with students:
    a. One student hides a small pocketbook around the room while another person hides their eyes in a corner. When the pocketbook is hidden, students start singing the song. If the student gets close to the pocketbook, students sing faster. If the student moves away from the pocketbook, students sing slower. When the student finds the book, he or she becomes the new hider! Instead of fast/slow you could also do loud/soft.
4. Have students practice identifying Mi, Sol, and La notes in song.
5. Instruct students to complete fun sheet on Mi, Sol, and La (Appendix A).

Assessment Tools
- Sing rubric (Appendix A).
- Identify Mi, Sol, and La paper assessment (Appendix A).

Lucy Locket

English Nursery Rhyme

Mi Sol La: The Cow Who Clucked

Objectives (with National Standards and National Core Arts Standards)
- Sing, alone and with others, a varied repertoire of music. (NS 1; NCAS 5.1)
- Use a system (solfège) to read simple pitch notation on the staff. (NS 5; NCAS 4.2)
- Understand relationships between music and disciplines outside the arts. (NS 8; NCAS 11)

Inter-disciplinary Connections
- Language Arts

Teaching Procedures
1. Introduce/review with students Mi, Sol, and La from *Pitch Hill*.
2. Introduce students to the book, *The Cow Who Clucked,* by Denise Flemming (ISBN: 978-0805072655).
3. Teach the song first on solfège, then with lyrics. Read the book and add the song after the phrase "And on she went."
4. Have students practice identifying Mi, Sol, and La.
5. Have students complete fun sheet on Mi, Sol, and La (Appendix A).

Assessment Tools
- Singing rubric (Appendix A).
- Identifying Mi, Sol, and La paper assessment (Appendix A).

The Cow Who Clucked

Shelley Tomich

Mi Sol La: It's Raining, It's Pouring

Objectives (with National Standards and National Core Arts Standards)
- Sing, alone and with others, a varied repertoire of music. (NS 1; NCAS 5.1)
- Perform on instruments in groups, matching dynamic levels, and responding to the cues of a conductor. (NS 2; NCAS 4.2; NCAS 5.1; NCAS 6.1)
- Improvise short instrumental pieces using a variety of sound sources including body sounds. (NS 3; NCAS 1)
- Use a system (solfège) to read simple pitch notation on the staff. (NS 5; NCAS 4.2)
- Understand relationships between music and disciplines outside the arts. (NS 8; NCAS 11)

Inter-disciplinary Connections
- Language Arts

Teaching Procedures
1. Introduce/review with students Mi, Sol, and La from Pitch Hill.
2. Sing through "Rain, Rain, Go Away."
3. Analyze song as a Sol-Mi song.
4. Teach, "It's Raining, It's Pouring" first on solfège, then with lyrics.
5. Analyze song as a Mi, Sol, and La song. Compare and contrast with the song, "Rain, Rain, Go Away."
6. Sing through the book *It's Raining, It's Pouring* by Kin Eagle (ISBN: 978-0613342926).
7. Complete fun sheet on Mi, Sol, and La (Appendix A).
8. Instruct students to create their own rainstorm using rain sticks, hand drums, and/or body percussion. Students can blow for wind sounds, snap to create a light rainstorm, clap for thunder, and pat for heavy rain. I start by having students slowly make the wind sound. Then we snap lightly and move to patting. Finally we clap hard for thunder and then do the motions in reverse. Students also can be the conductor of the class rainstorm.

Assessment Tools
- Singing rubric (Appendix A).
- Performing on Instruments rubric (Appendix A).
- Identifying Mi, Sol, and La paper assessment (Appendix A).

Rain, Rain, Go Away

English Nursery Rhyme

Rain, rain, go a-way! Come a-gain a-noth-er day!

It's Raining, It's Pouring

Traditional

It's rain-ing, it's pour-ing, The old man is snor-ing. Went to bed and he

bumped his head, and he could-n't get up in the morn-ing!

Do Mi Sol La: Apple Tree

Objectives (with National Standards and National Core Arts Standards)
- Sing, alone and with others, a varied repertoire of music. (NS 1; NCAS 5.1)
- Perform on instruments, alone and with others, a varied repertoire of music. (NS 2; NCAS 4.2; NCAS 5.1)
- Use a system (solfège) to read simple pitch notation on the staff. (NS 5; NCAS 4.2)
- Understand relationships between music and disciplines outside the arts. (NS 8; NCAS 11)

Inter-disciplinary Connections
- Science

Teaching Procedures
1. Introduce/review with students Do, Mi, Sol, and La from *Pitch Hill*.
2. Teach traditional game song "Apple Tree" first on solfège, then with lyrics. Emphasize Do as the lowest and final note in this song.
3. As part of connections to science, discuss Sir Isaac Newton and the theory of the falling apple.
4. Have students play simple xylophone accompaniment on F and C (take other bars off).
5. Play game with students:
    a. Have students stand in a circle with one person holding a beanbag (apple) in the middle as the tree. Students in the circle walk in one direction while singing the song while the person in the middle spins in the other direction. On the word "out," the person in the middle gently lets go of their beanbag, and it will land close to another student. This student is the new tree and the previous tree stands off to the side to be a member of the singing forest. Alternatively, you could have students play an instrument once they are out.
6. Complete fun sheet on Do, Mi, Sol and La (Appendix A).

Assessment Tools
- Singing rubric (Appendix A).
- Performing on Instruments rubric (Appendix A).
- Identifying Do, Mi, Sol, and La paper assessment (Appendix A).

Apple Tree

Traditional Game Song

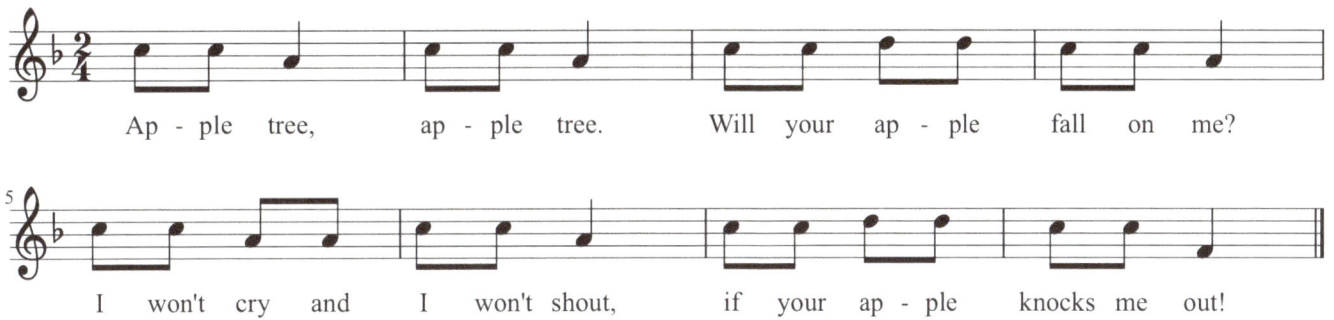

Do Re Mi: Hiccup Buttercup

Objectives (with National Standards and National Core Arts Standards)
- Sing, alone and with others, a varied repertoire of music. (NS 1; NCAS 5.1)
- Perform easy rhythm patterns on instruments in groups while maintaining a steady tempo. (NS 2; NCAS 4.2; NCAS 5.1)
- Use a system (solfège) to read simple pitch notation on the staff. (NS 5; NCAS 4.2)

Teaching Procedures
1. Introduce/review with students Do, Re, and Mi from *Pitch Hill.*
2. Teach song first on solfège, then with lyrics.
3. Play cup game with students using plastic cups:
    a. Sit in a circle with students with a cup upside down in front of them.
    b. Complete the following movements:
        1. Hiccup, Buttercup = Clap Clap, Tap Tap Tap (on cup)
        2. Flies, all – grab cup, flip over
        3. Night – place cup
        4. Take, your – clap, grab cup
        5. Cup – tap cup in other hand
        6. And – put down on floor (upside down – flipping the cup)
        7. Pass, it – clap, grab
        8. Right – put it in front of person to your right.
4. Practice identifying Do, Re, and Mi on the music staff.
5. Complete fun sheet on Do Re Mi (Appendix A).

Assessment Tools
- Singing rubric (Appendix A).
- Performing on Instruments rubric (Appendix A).
- Identifying Do, Re, and Mi paper assessment (Appendix A).

Hiccup Buttercup

Shelley Tomich

Hic - cup But-ter-cup, flies all night, Take your cup and pass it right!

Do Re Mi: Froggy Learns to Swim

Objectives (with National Standards and National Core Arts Standards)
- Sing, alone and with others, a varied repertoire of music. (NS 1; NCAS 5.1)
- Use a system (solfège) to read simple pitch notation on the staff. (NS 5; NCAS 4.2)
- Respond through purposeful movement (choreography) to specific music events. (NS 6; NCAS 4.2; NCAS 4.3; NCAS 5; NCAS 6; NCAS 8)
- Understand relationships between music and disciplines outside the arts. (NS 8; NCAS 11)

Inter-disciplinary Connections
- Language Arts

Teaching Procedures
1. Introduce/review with students Do, Re, and Mi from *Pitch Hill*.
2. Introduce the book *Froggy Learns to Swim* by Jonathan London and Frank Remkieweicz (ISBN: 0-613-02825-2).
3. As part of the book, the character "Froggy" will learn the song and use it to learn how to swim.
4. As students perform the song, they can add the following choreography (Chicken, Airplane, Soldier sequence will make a swimming motion):
    a. Bubble – Bubble: pretend to blow bubbles down low.
    b. Toot-Toot: raise hands in air twice.
    c. Chicken: Raise elbows up in traditional "chicken" stance.
    d. Airplane: Arms straight out from side.
    e. Soldier: Arms straight down from side.
5. Complete fun sheet on Do, Re, and Mi (Appendix A).

Assessment Tools
- Singing rubric (Appendix A).
- Identifying Do, Re, and Mi paper assessment (Appendix A).

Froggy Learns to Swim

Jonathan London

arr. Shelley Tomich

Do Re Mi: Ten Little Fish

Objectives (with National Standards and Core Arts Standards)
- Sing, alone and with others, a varied repertoire of music. (NS 1; NCAS 5.1)
- Arrange short songs within specified guidelines. (NS 4; NCAS 2; NCAS 3.1; NCAS 3.2)
- Use a system (solfège) to read simple pitch notation on the staff. (NS 5; NCAS 4.2)
- Identify simple music forms when presented aurally. (NS 6; NS 4.2)
- Use appropriate terminology in explaining music and music performances. (NS 6; NCAS 4.2)
- Understand relationships between music and disciplines outside the arts. (NS 8; NCAS 11)
- Demonstrate audience behavior appropriate for the context and style of music performed. (NS 9; NCAS 6)

Inter-disciplinary Connections
- Language Arts
- Math

Teaching Procedures
1. Introduce/review with students Do, Re, and Mi from *Pitch Hill*.
2. Discuss lyrics and the various methods composers use to write lyrics.
3. Read/sing the book *Ten Little Fish* by Audrey Wood (ISBN: 978-0439635691).
4. Show students the fun sheet (following page) and explain how to complete it (the arrow pointing to the blank has to rhyme with the circled number). You can either have them do the full ten verses or simplify to five. Complete a class song and then have students complete the sheet themselves or in a small group.
5. Have students review the pitches of the song and then perform the song for the class using their own lyrics.
6. Have students complete fun sheet on Do, Re, and Mi (Appendix A).

Assessment Tools
- Singing rubric (Appendix A).
- Ten Little Fish Composing Lyrics Papers (pages 35-36).
- Identifying Do, Re, and Mi paper assessment (Appendix A).

Little Fish Composition

Name: _____

Five little _____ _____ _____

One _____ and now there are (four!) ↗

Four little _____ _____ _____

One _____ and now there are (three!) ↗

Three little _____ _____ _____

One _____ and now there are (two!) ↗

Two little _____ _____ _____

One _____ and now there is (one!) ↗

One little _____ _____ _____

One _____ and now there are (none!) ↗

Ten Little Fish

Audrey Wood

arr. Shelley Tomich

Ten lit-tle fish, swim-ing in a line, One dives down and now there are nine!

Little Fish Composition

Name: _____

Ten little _____ _____ _____

One _____ and now there are (nine!) →

Nine little _____ _____ _____

One _____ and now there are (eight!) →

Eight little _____ _____ _____

One _____ and now there are (seven!) →

Seven little _____ _____ _____

One _____ and now there are (six!) →

Six little _____ _____ _____

One _____ and now there are (five!) →

Five little _____ _____ _____

One _____ and now there are (four!) →

Four little _____ _____ _____

One _____ and now there are (three!) →

Three little _____ _____ _____

One _____ and now there are (two!) →

Two little _____ _____ _____

One _____ and now there is (one!) →

One little _____ _____ _____

One _____ and now there are (none!) →

Do Re Mi Sol La: 'Round and 'Round

Objectives (with National Standards and Core Arts Standards)
- Sing from memory a varied repertoire of songs representing genres and styles from diverse cultures. (NS 1; NCAS 5.1)
- Use a system (solfège) to read simple pitch notation on the staff. (NS 5; NCAS 4.2)
- Identify various uses of music in daily experiences. (NS 9; NCAS 10; NCAS 11)
- Understand relationships between music and disciplines outside the arts. (NS 8; NCAS 11)

Inter-disciplinary Connections
- Social Studies

Teaching Procedures
1. Introduce/review with students Do, Re, Mi, Sol, and La from *Pitch Hill*.
2. Introduce song from the West Indies and discuss where the West Indies are located.
3. Discuss singing games and how they play an important part of daily life in rural areas.
4. Teach "Round and Round" first on solfège, then with lyrics.
5. Teach game:
   a. Students stand in a large circle and hold onto a stretchy band (I purchased mine at http://bearpawcreek.com). When students let go of it, it flies across the room and "hits" a student or group of students - don't worry – it doesn't hurt! Students sing the song while walking in a circle with the stretchy band. On the final "Bom" of the song, let go of the stretchy band, and the person(s) the band wraps around is out.
6. Practice identifying Do, Re, Mi, Sol, and La on the music staff.
7. Complete fun sheet on Do, Re, Mi, Sol, and La (Appendix A).

Assessment Tools
- Singing rubric (Appendix A).
- Identifying Do, Re, Mi, Sol, and La paper assessment (Appendix A).

'Round and 'Round

Game Song from St. Kitts, West Indies

Do Re Mi Sol La: Mañana Iguana

Objectives (with National Standards and National Core Arts Standards)
- Sing, alone and with others, a varied repertoire of music. (NS 1; NCAS 5.1)
- Sing from memory a varied repertoire of songs representing genres and styles from diverse cultures. (NS 1; NCAS 5.1; NCAS 4.3)
- Perform easy rhythmic patterns accurately on classroom instruments. (NS 2; NCAS 4.2; NCAS 5.1)
- Use a system (solfège) to read simple pitch notation on the staff. (NS 5; NCAS 4.2)
- Identify the sounds of a variety of instruments from various cultures. (NS 6; NCAS 4.2; NCAS 8)
- Understand relationships between music and disciplines outside the arts. (NS 8; NCAS 11)

Inter-disciplinary Connections
- Language Arts
- Social Studies

Teaching Procedures
1. Introduce/review with students Do, Re, Mi, Sol, and La from *Pitch Hill.*
2. Teach students the song "Mañana Iguana" first on solfège, then with lyrics.
3. Add two snaps on the two rest beats after "say" and "late." Transfer snaps to castanets (or other non-pitched percussion instruments). If using castanets, discuss why they would be an appropriate instrument choice for the song, "Mañana Iguana."
4. Introduce the book *Mañana Iguana* by Ann Whitford Paul (ISBN: 978-0823418084). Discuss some of the Spanish words found in the book (the book translates them at the beginning of the book) and the geographical origin of these words.
5. Read the book and add the song after the phrase "and she did' each time it occurs in the book.
6. Complete fun sheet on Do, Re, Mi, Sol, and La for Mañana Iguana (Appendix A).

Assessment Tools
- Singing rubric (Appendix A).
- Performing on Instruments rubric (Appendix A).
- Identifying Do, Re, Mi, Sol, and La paper assessment (Appendix A).

Mañana Iguana

Shelley Tomich

"Man - añ - a I - gua - na," is what they say.

Man - añ - a I - gua - na, will be too late!

Do Re Mi Sol La: Rainbow Fish

Objectives (with National Standards and National Core Arts Standards)
- Sing, alone and with others, a varied repertoire of music. (NS 1; NCAS 5.1)
- Sing from memory a varied repertoire of songs representing genres and styles from diverse cultures. (NS 1; NCAS 5.1; NCAS 4.3)
- Perform easy rhythm patterns on instruments in groups while maintaining a steady tempo. (NS 2; NCAS 4.2; NCAS 5.1; NCAS 6.1)
- Use a system (solfège) to read simple pitch notation on the staff. (NS 5; NCAS 4.2)
- Demonstrate perceptual skills by moving, by answering questions about, and by describing aural examples of music of various styles. (NS 6; NCAS 4.3; NCAS 8.1)
- Respond through purposeful movement to selected prominent music characteristics or specific music events while listening to music.
(NS 6; NCAS 4.2; NCAS 4.3; NCAS 5; NCAS 6; NCAS 8)
- Understand relationships between music and disciplines outside the arts.
(NS 8; NCAS 11)

Inter-disciplinary Connections
- Language Arts
- Science

Teaching Procedures
1. Introduce/review with students Do, Re, Mi, Sol, and La from *Pitch Hill* (may want to do this step after steps 2 and 3).
2. Have students listen to Camille Saint-Saëns' *Aquarium* from *The Carnival of the Animals.*
3. Identify sound as fish-inspired music.
4. Pass out fish puppets or scarves and have students create appropriate movements to match the music. Alternatively, have students move like fish (do four half note steps swaying with scarves and then do a ¼ turn counterclockwise like a school of fish).
5. Introduce the book *Rainbow Fish* by Marcus Pfister (ISBN: 978-1558580091).
6. Teach song first on solfège, then with lyrics.
7. Teach students a simple xylophone accompaniment (I use half notes) on F and C (take other bars off).
8. Have students perform the song as you read the book again.
9. Complete fun sheet on Do, Re, Mi, Sol, and La (Appendix A).

Assessment Tools
- Singing rubric (Appendix A) and Performing on Instruments rubric (Appendix A).
- Identifying Do, Re, Mi, Sol, and La paper assessment (Appendix A).

PITCH HILL

Rainbow Fish

Charlie Tighe
arr. Shelley Tomich

"Der Regenbogenfisch" by Marcus Pfister
© 1992 NordSüd Verlag AG, Zurich/ Switzerland

Do Re Mi Sol La: I Have a Car

Objectives (with National Standards and National Core Arts Standards)
- Sing, alone and with others, a varied repertoire of music. (NS 1; NCAS 5.1)
- Perform easy rhythmic patterns accurately and independently on classroom instruments. (NS 2; NCAS 4.2; NCAS 5.1; NCAS 6.1)
- Use a system (solfège) to read simple pitch notation on the staff. (NS 5; NCAS 4.2)
- Identify simple music forms when presented aurally. (NS 6; NS 4.2)
- Respond through purposeful movement to specific music events while listening to music. (NS 6; NCAS 4.2; NCAS 4.3; NCAS 5; NCAS 6; NCAS 8)
- Identify various uses of music in daily experiences. (NS 9; NCAS 10; NCAS 11)

Teaching Procedures
1. Introduce/review with students Do, Re, Mi, Sol, and La from *Pitch Hill*.
2. Introduce the song to students and discuss what a "rumble seat" is.
3. Sing first on solfège, then with lyrics.
4. Compare and contrast the two sections of the song.
5. Teach students simple choreography:
    a. During the first section, students should pretend to drive a car.
    b. During the second section, students should perform the following movements:
        i. Honk – Do the tug-down motion with your hand in a fist (like you used to as a kid to get big trucks to honk at you!).
        ii. Rattle – Jazz Hand Shake
        iii. Crash – Clap
        iv. Beep – make a beeping motion In the air with palm of your hand
6. Sing the song with choreography.
7. Add hand drums and use them as steering wheels in section one, and then play the second section as a pattern on the drum.
8. Practice identifying Do, Re, Mi, Sol, and La on the music staff.
9. Complete fun sheet on Do, Re, Mi, Sol, and La (Appendix A).

Assessment Tools
- Singing rubric (Appendix A).
- Performing on Instruments rubric (Appendix A).
- Identifying Do, Re, Mi, Sol, and La paper assessment (Appendix A).

PITCH HILL

I Have a Car

Traditional

I have a car, it's made of tin. No-bod-y know what shape it's in! It has four wheels and a rum-ble seat, Hear us chug-ging down the street! Honk, honk, rat-tle, rat-tle, rat-tle, crash, beep, beep! Honk, honk, rat-tle, rat-tle, rat-tle, crash, beep, beep! Honk, honk, rat-tle, rat-tle, rat-tle, crash, beep, beep! Honk! Honk!

RUMBLE SEAT

Do Re Mi Fa: Silly Sally

Objectives (with National Standards and National Core Arts Standards)
- Sing, alone and with others, a varied repertoire of music. (NS 1; NCAS 5.1)
- Perform chord patterns accurately on classroom instruments. (NS 2; NCAS 4.2; NCAS 5.1)
- Arrange music to accompany readings or dramatizations. (NS 4; NCAS 2.1)
- Use a system (solfège) to read simple pitch notation on the staff. (NS 5; NCAS 4.2)
- Understand relationships between music and disciplines outside the arts. (NS 8; NCAS 11)

Inter-disciplinary Connections
- Language Arts

Teaching Procedures
1. Introduce/review with students Do, Re, Mi, and Fa from *Pitch Hill*.
2. Teach students the song "Silly Sally" first on solfège, then with lyrics.
3. Set up xylophones with F, C and Bb bars only.
4. Have students play xylophone steady beat accompaniment on F/C. On the word "town" we switch to F/Bb and then back to F/C on "walking." We briefly discuss why we have to make this change.
5. Introduce the book *Silly Sally* by Audrey Wood (ISBN: 978-0152744281).
6. Read the book and have students sing song, changing the "action verb" each time.
7. Complete fun sheet on Do Re Mi Fa (Silly Sally). Early finishers can use the fun sheet on the following page to illustrate their new "ing" action.
8. Sing and perform the new verses composed by students.

Assessment Tools
- Singing rubric (Appendix A).
- Performing on Instruments rubric (Appendix A).
- Identifying Do, Re, Mi, and Fa "Silly Sally" paper assessment (Appendix A).

Silly Sally

Audrey Wood   Shelley Tomich

Name: _____

Directions: Write in your "ing" verb in the space at the bottom of the page. Draw a picture of Sally performing your "ing" verb.

Silly Sally Illustration

Today in music class we sang a song about "Silly Sally."
She found silly ways to get to town!

Silly Sally went to town, _____ backwards upside down!

Mi Fa Sol La: Over in the Meadow

Objectives (with National Standards and National Core Arts Standards)
- Sing, alone and with others, a varied repertoire of music. (NS 1; NCAS 5.1)
- Use a system (solfège) to read simple pitch notation on the staff. (NS 5; NCAS 4.2)
- Understand relationships between music and disciplines outside the arts. (NS 8; NCAS 11)

Inter-disciplinary Connections
- Language Arts
- Math

Teaching Procedures
1. Introduce/review with students Do, Re, Mi, Fa, and Sol from *Pitch Hill*.
2. Teach students the song "Over in the Meadow" first on solfège, then with lyrics.
3. Sing through the book *Over in the Meadow* by Olive A. Wadsworth and Ezra Jack Keats (ISBN: 978-0590448482).
4. Sing through *Over in the Garden* by Jennifer Ward (ISBN: 978-0873587938). The lyrics are different from "Over in the Meadow," but the melody is the same. We compare and contrast the two storybooks. Students can practice picking out the numbers and animals hidden in each illustration. Jennifer Ward included the melody with her altered lyrics in the back of her book.
5. Practice identifying Do, Re, Mi, Fa, Sol, and La on the music staff.
6. Complete fun sheet on Do, Re, Mi, Fa, Sol, and La (Appendix A).

Assessment Tools
- Singing rubric (Appendix A).
- Identifying Do, Re, Mi, Sol, and La paper assessment (Appendix A).

Over in the Meadow

Olive A. Wadsworth

Over in the meadow,
Where the stream runs blue
Lived an old mother fish
And her little fishes two.
"Swim!" said the mother;
"We swim!" said the two,
So they swam and they leaped
Where the stream runs blue.

Over in the meadow,
In a snug beehive
Lived a mother honey bee
And her little bees five.
"Buzz!" said the mother;
"We buzz!" said the five
So they buzzed and they hummed
In the snug beehive.

Over in the meadow,
By the old mossy gate
Lived a brown mother lizard
And her little lizards eight.
"Bask!" said the mother;
"We bask!" said the eight
So they basked in the sun
On the old mossy gate.

Over in the meadow,
In a hole in a tree
Lived an old mother bluebird
And her little birdies three.
"Sing!" said the mother;
"We sing!" said the three
So they sang and were glad
In a hole in the tree.

Over in the meadow,
In a nest built of sticks
Lived a black mother crow
And her little crows six
"Caw!" said the mother;
"We caw!" said the six.
So they cawed and they called
In their nest built of sticks.

Over in the meadow,
Where the quiet pools shine
Lived a green mother frog
And her little froggies nine.
"Croak!" said the mother;
"We croak!" said the nine
So they croaked and they splashed
Where the quiet pools shine.

Over in the meadow,
In the reeds on the shore
Lived an old mother muskrat
And her little ratties four.
"Dive!" said the mother;
"We dive!" said the four
So they dived and they burrowed
In the reeds on the shore.

Over in the meadow,
Where the grass is so even
Lived a gay mother cricket
And her little crickets seven.
"Chirp!" said the mother;
"We chirp!" said the seven
So they chirped cheery notes
In the grass soft and even.

Over in the meadow,
In a sly little den
Lived a gray mother spider
And her little spiders ten.
"Spin!" said the mother;
"We spin!" said the ten
So they spun lacy webs
In their sly little den.

Low-Sol Do Re Mi Fa Sol La:
Fish and Chips and Vinegar

Objectives (with National Standards and National Core Arts Standards)
- Sing, alone and with others, a varied repertoire of music. (NS 1; NCAS 5.1)
- Sing from memory a varied repertoire of songs representing genres and styles from diverse cultures. (NS 1; NCAS 5.1; NCAS 4.3)
- Use a system (solfège) to read simple pitch notation on the staff. (NS 5; NCAS 4.2)
- Respond through purposeful movement (choreography) to specific music events. (NS 6; NCAS 4.2; NCAS 4.3; NCAS 5; NCAS 6; NCAS 8)
- Identify various uses of music in daily experiences. (NS 9; NCAS 10; NCAS 11)
- Understand relationships between music and disciplines outside the arts. (NS 8; NCAS 11)

Inter-disciplinary Connections
- Social Studies

Teaching Procedures
1. Introduce/review with students Do, Re, Mi, Fa, Sol, and La from *Pitch Hill.* Introduce Low Sol by showing him standing on his head!
2. Teach students the song "Fish and Chips and Vinegar" first on solfège, then with lyrics. Discuss what "fish and chips" are.
3. Have students perform each section individually and then as a round.
4. Add choreography:
    a. Section 1 – Step forward measure 1, back measure 2, forward, back, etc. and jump up at the end on "pop."
    b. Section 2 – Stand with one hand on hip and with other hand use the index finger to point at students and "sass" them (students love this!).
    c. Stand with hands clasped together at chest level with elbows point out (think classic caroling stance) and sway back and forth. On "pepper" pretend to shake out the pepper and throw hands in the air for salt.
5. Practice identifying Do, Re, Mi, Fa, Sol and La on the music staff.
6. Complete fun sheet on Do, Re, Mi, Fa, Sol, and La (Appendix A).

Assessment Tools
- Singing rubric (Appendix A).
- Identifying Do, Re, Mi, Sol, and La paper assessment (Appendix A).

Fish and Chips and Vinegar

Traditional

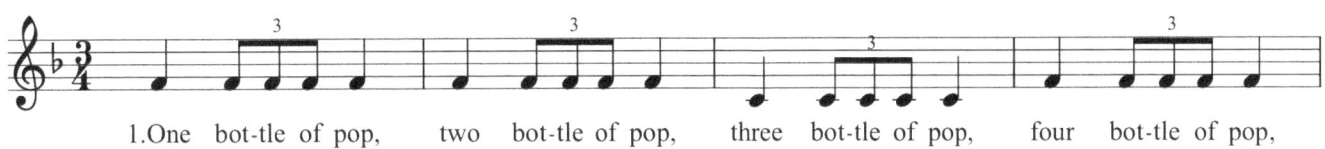
1. One bottle of pop, two bottle of pop, three bottle of pop, four bottle of pop,

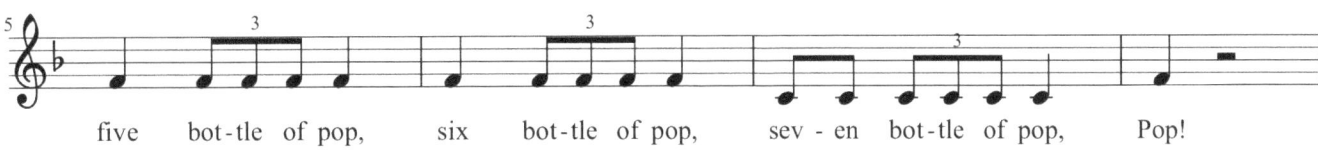
five bottle of pop, six bottle of pop, seven bottle of pop, Pop!

2. Don't throw your junk in my back-yard, my back-yard, my back-yard.

Don't throw your junk in my back-yard, my back-yard's full!

3. Fish and chips and vinegar, vinegar, vinegar, Fish and chips and

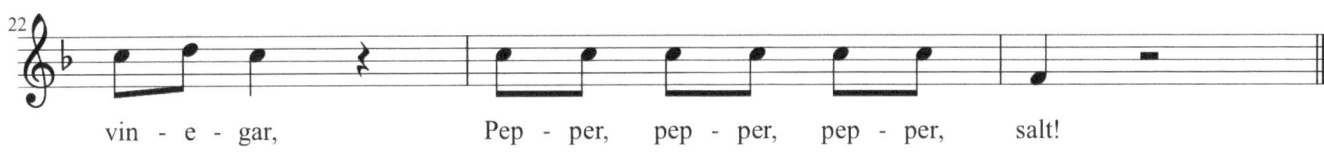
vinegar, Pepper, pepper, pepper, salt!

Low-Sol Do Re Mi Fa Sol La: Frère Jacques

Objectives (with National Standards and National Core Arts Standards)
- Sing, alone and with others, a varied repertoire of music including rounds. (NS 1; NCAS 5.1)
- Sing from memory a varied repertoire of songs representing genres and styles from diverse cultures. (NS 1; NCAS 5.1; NCAS 4.3)
- Use a system (solfège) to read simple pitch notation on the staff. (NS 5; NCAS 4.2)
- Respond through purposeful movement (choreography) to specific music events. (NS 6; NCAS 4.2; NCAS 4.3; NCAS 5; NCAS 6; NCAS 8)
- Understand relationships between music and disciplines outside the arts. (NS 8; NCAS 11)

Inter-disciplinary Connections
- Social Studies

Teaching Procedures
1. Introduce/review with students Do, Re, Mi, Fa, Sol, and La from *Pitch Hill*. Introduce Low Sol by showing him standing on his head!
2. Play 'guess the song' game by singing, "Twinkle, Twinkle, Little Star" and "Mary Had a Little Lamb" on solfège, and have students guess the melody. Sing "Frère Jacques" and see if any students can guess the melody of this song.
3. Teach students the song "Frère Jacques" first on solfège, then English, then French lyrics.
4. Practice the song as a round. I begin by trying to "trick" students into "messing up" by having them start the round and then I come in. Once students identify what I am doing, we practice performing the round as a class.
5. Teach choreography:
    a. Students stand in a circle, join hands, and move in one direction around the circle on m.1 and m.2. Go the opposite way on m.3 and m.4. Then have students stop and pretend to ring bells in place on m.5 and m.6. Finally, students will turn in a circle in place on m.7 and m.8.
6. Perform the song complete with the choreography as a round.
7. Complete fun sheet on Do Re Mi Fa Sol and La (Appendix A).

Assessment Tools
- Singing rubric (Appendix A) and Performing on Instruments rubric (Appendix A).
- Identifying Do, Re, Mi, Sol, and La paper assessment (Appendix A).

Frère Jacques

French Folk Song

Low-Sol Low-La Do Re Mi Fa Sol La:
The Very Lazy Ladybug

Objectives (with National Standards and National Core Arts Standards)
- Sing, alone and with others, a varied repertoire of music. (NS 1; NCAS 5.1)
- Perform chord patterns accurately on classroom instruments. (NS 2; NCAS 4.2; NCAS 5.1)
- Use a system (solfège) to read simple pitch notation on the staff. (NS 5; NCAS 4.2)
- Understand relationships between music and disciplines outside the arts. (NS 8; NCAS 11)

Inter-disciplinary Connections
- Language Arts

Teaching Procedures
1. Introduce/review Do, Re, Mi, Fa, Sol, La, Low-Sol, and Low-La using *Pitch Hill*.
2. Introduce the book, *The Very Lazy Ladybug** by Isobel Finn (ISBN: 978-1589255104).
3. Teach the song first on solfège, then with lyrics.
4. Teach students a steady beat xylophone accompaniment on G and D.
5. Sing the song with the book performing after each new animal experience.
6. Complete fun sheet on Do, Re, Mi, Sol, and La (Appendix A).

Assessment Tools
- Singing rubric (Appendix A).
- Performing on Instruments rubric (Appendix A).
- Identifying Do, Re, Mi, Sol, and La paper assessment (Appendix A).

The Very Lazy Ladybug

arr. Shelley Tomich

*Published by Tiger Tales

Do Re Mi Fa Sol La Ti SD: Do-do Bird

Objectives (with National Standards and National Core Arts Standards)
- Sing, alone and with others, a varied repertoire of music. (NS 1; NCAS 5.1)
- Use a system (solfège) to read simple pitch notation on the staff. (NS 5; NCAS 4.2)
- Identify the sounds of a variety of instruments including children's voices and male/female adult voices. (NS 6; NCAS 4.2; NCAS 8)
- Understand relationships between music and disciplines outside the arts. (NS 8; NCAS 11)
- Identify and describe roles of musicians in various music settings and cultures. (NS 9; NCAS 11)

Inter-disciplinary Connections
- Social Studies

Teaching Procedures
1. Introduce/review with students Do, Re, Mi, Fa, Sol, La, Ti, and SD from Pitch Hill.
2. Read the book *Do Re Mi: If You Can Read Music, Thank Guido D'Arezzo* by Susan Roth (ISBN: 0618465723).
3. Discuss with students how solfège notes were first written down according to the story.
4. Play the Do-Do Bird game.
    a. Explain what a Do-do bird is (bird who went extinct a really long time ago).
    b. Write the pattern "Mi-do-do" on the board.
    c. Explain to students you will sing a simple 4 beat pattern and they should sing it back *unless* it is the pattern "Mi-do-do." If you sing this "extinct" pattern, then they should stay silent.
    d. Start with all students standing and have them sit down once they are out. As the game progresses, add additional extinct patterns to the board.
5. Practice identifying Do, Re, Mi, Fa, Sol, La, Ti, and SD on the music staff.
6. Complete fun sheet on Do, Re, Mi, Fa, Sol, La, Ti, and SD (Appendix A).

Assessment Tools
- Singing rubric (Appendix A).
- Identifying Do, Re, Mi, Fa, Sol, La, Ti, and SD paper assessment (Appendix A).

Do Re Mi Fa Sol La Ti SD: Pick-a-Pumpkin

Objectives (with National Standards and National Core Arts Standards)
- Sing, alone and with others, a varied repertoire of music. (NS 1; NCAS 5.1)
- Perform easy rhythmic patterns on classroom instruments. (NS 2; NCAS 4.2; NCAS 5.1)
- Use a system (solfège) to read simple pitch notation on the staff. (NS 5; NCAS 4.2)
- Identify various uses of music in their daily experiences and describe characteristics that make certain music suitable for each use. (NS 9; NCAS 10; NCAS 11)

Teaching Procedures

1. Introduce/review with students Do, Re, Mi, Fa, Sol, La, Ti, and SD from Pitch Hill.
2. Teach song first on solfège, then with lyrics. Note: words altered from traditional version to allow students who cannot participate in direct Halloween activities. I have included both the new and original texts on the following page.
3. I teach students to play the rhythm of the words on non-pitched instruments.
4. Play game with song:
    a. Take a beanbag or a small pumpkin and pass it around the circle. When the song is over, whoever is left with the beanbag is out. When a student is out, they go back to playing the non-pitched rhythm part.
5. Practice identifying Do, Re, Mi, Fa, Sol, La, Ti, and SD on the music staff.
6. Complete fun sheet on Do, Re, Mi, Fa, Sol, La, Ti, and SD (Appendix A).

Assessment Tools
- Singing rubric (Appendix A).
- Performing on Instruments rubric (Appendix A).
- Identifying Do, Re, Mi, Sol, and La paper assessment (Appendix A).

PITCH HILL

Pick-a-Pumpkin

Naomi Caldwelll

Pick-a-Pumpkin

Naomi Caldwell
arr. Shelley Tomich

Appendix A: Rubrics and Fun Sheets

By purchasing this book you have permission to reproduce the student assessment papers on pages 35-36 and Appendix A for your students, even if you teach in more than one school. If one school has two or more teachers, one book may be shared in that one school only.

Blank templates are provided for you to create your own pitch patterns for your students. In addition, the blank templates can be used for students to compose their own *Pitch Hill* patterns.

Additional fun sheets and other resources can be purchased at www.PitchHill.com.

Name: _____

Rubric for Singing

	Beginning	Needs Developing	Proficient	Exemplary
Pitch	• Uses non-singing voice and/or • Cannot maintain pitch.	• Uses singing voice appropriately at least some of the time. • Has difficulty maintaining pitch consistently.	• Uses singing voice appropriately most of the time. • Maintains pitch for simple melodies. • Has trouble maintaining pitch for complex melodies.	• Uses singing voice appropriately all of the time. • Consistently maintains pitch for both simple and complex melodies.
Rhythm	• Tempo is incorrect or fluctuates inappropriately for song. • Rhythm is uncertain and/or incorrect.	• Has difficulty maintaining appropriate tempo consistently. • Rhythm is correct at least some of the time.	• Maintains tempo most of the time. • Rhythm is correct for songs with simple rhythm patterns. • Has trouble with more complex rhythm patterns.	• Maintains appropriate tempo all of the time. • Consistently performs correct rhythm patterns for both simple and complex songs.
Dynamics	• Dynamic level is often too loud, overpowering others, or so soft the song cannot be heard.	• Dynamic level varies inconsistently.	• Dynamic levels are consistent and generally appropriate to the song.	• Dynamics are appropriate for song and reflects notation or conductor's instructions.
Expression	• Has inappropriate or non-existent expression.	• Expression is appropriate some of the time.	• Expression is generally appropriate to the song.	• Expression enhances performance by adding appropriate depth and emotional range.

Comments: _____

Name: _____

Rubric for Playing Instruments

	Beginning	Needs Developing	Proficient	Exemplary
Instrument Technique	• Technique is improper. • Technique interferes with technical aspect of performance.	• Demonstrates proper technique some of the time. • Technique interferes with technical aspect of performance.	• Demonstrates proper technique most of the time. • Technique does not interfere with technical aspect of performance.	• Demonstrates proper technique all of the time.
Technical Aspect	• Pitch and/or rhythm is incorrect. • The song or pattern is unrecognizable.	• Pitch and/or rhythm is inconsistent. • At times the song or pattern is unrecognizable.	• Pitch and/or rhythm is correct most of the time. • Though mistakes occur, they are infrequent and do not hinder overall performance.	• Pitch and/or rhythm is consistently correct.
Respect of Instruments	• Does not show respect for instruments.	• Demonstrates proper care and handling of the instruments some of the time.	• Demonstrates proper care and handling of the instruments most of the time.	• Demonstrates proper care and handling of the instruments all of the time. • Serves as role model to other students

Comments: _____

PITCH HILL

Name: _____

Lines and Spaces

Write L for Line and S for Space

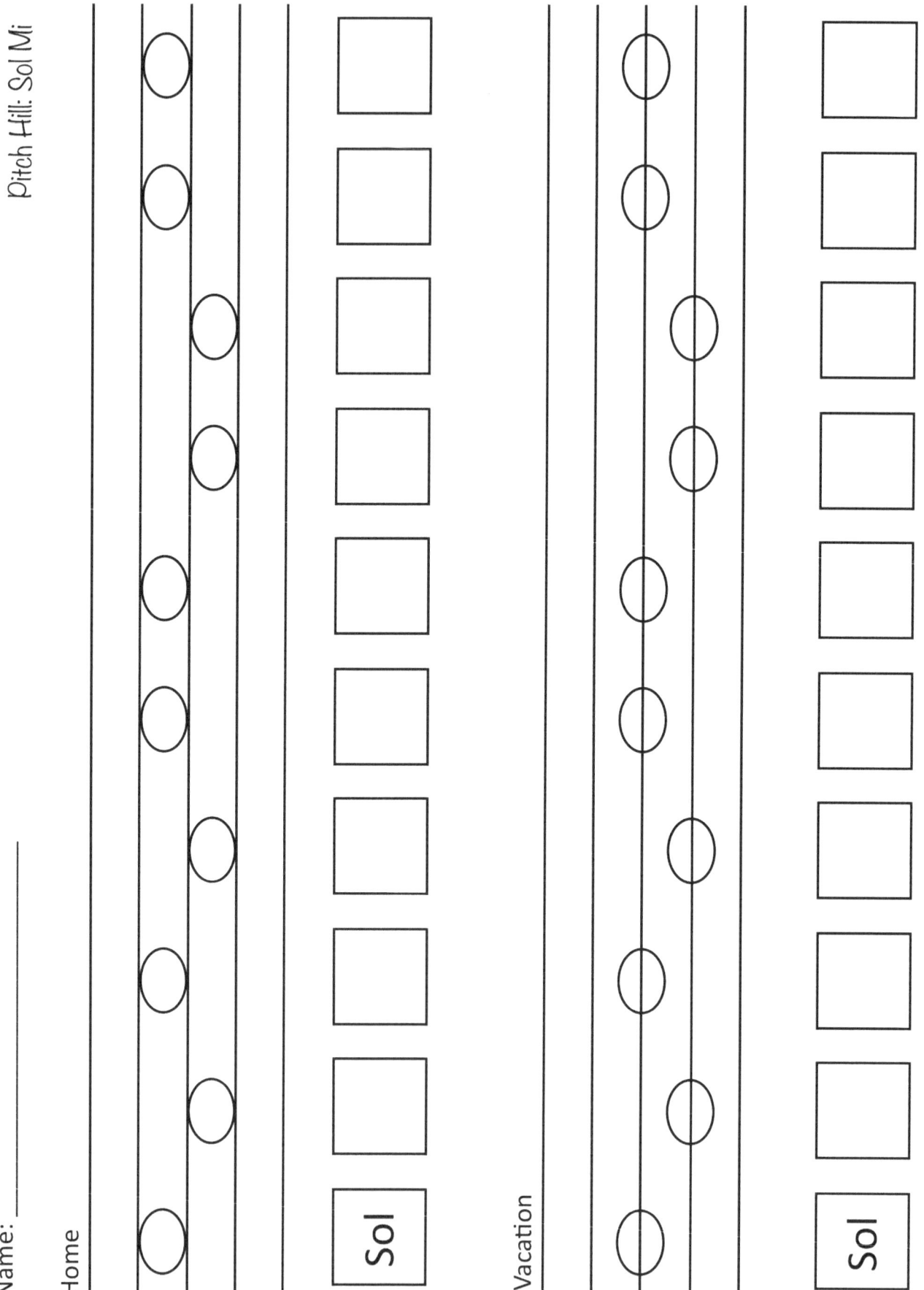

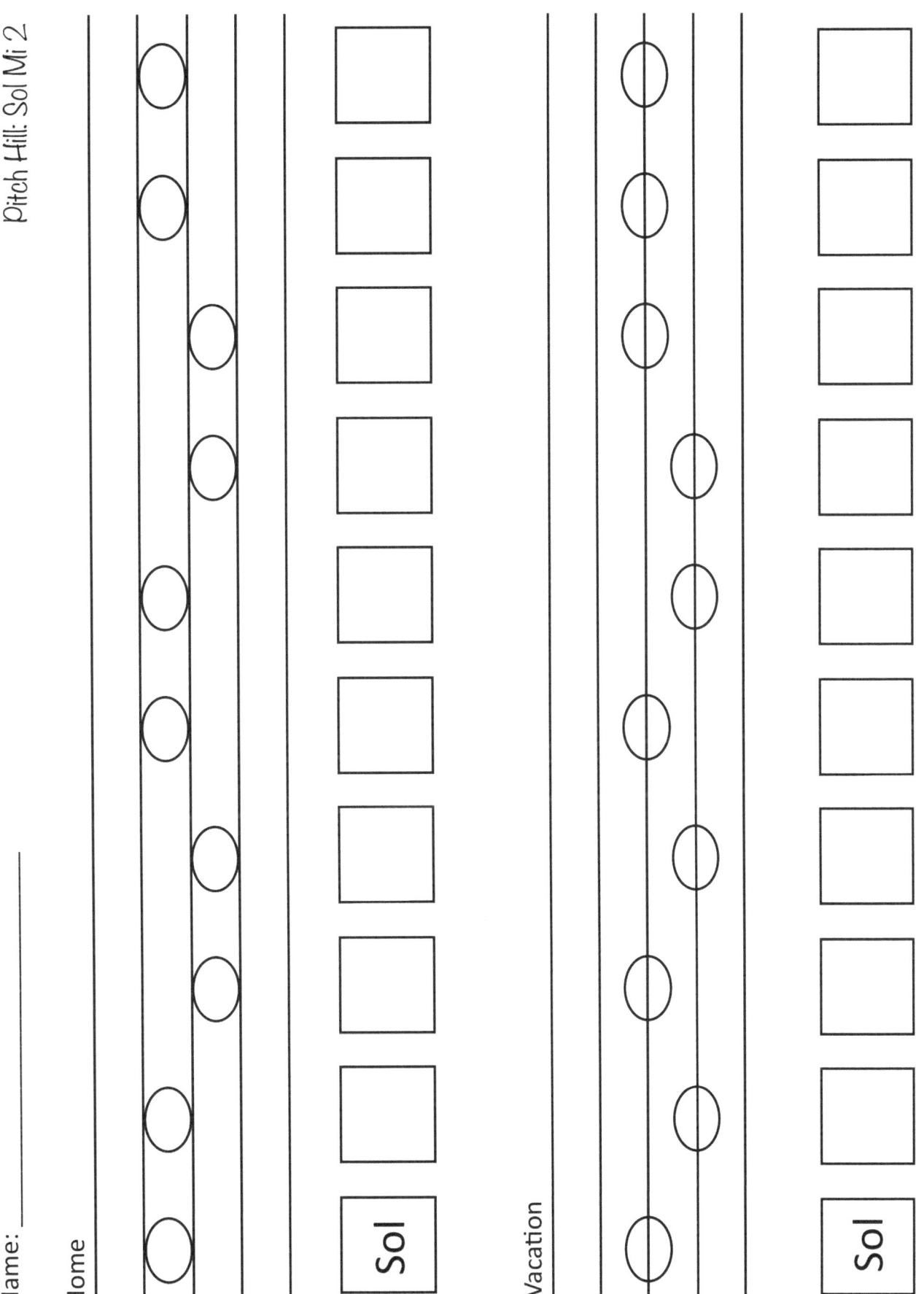

Pitch Hill: Mi Sol La

Name: _____

Home

Sol

Vacation

Sol

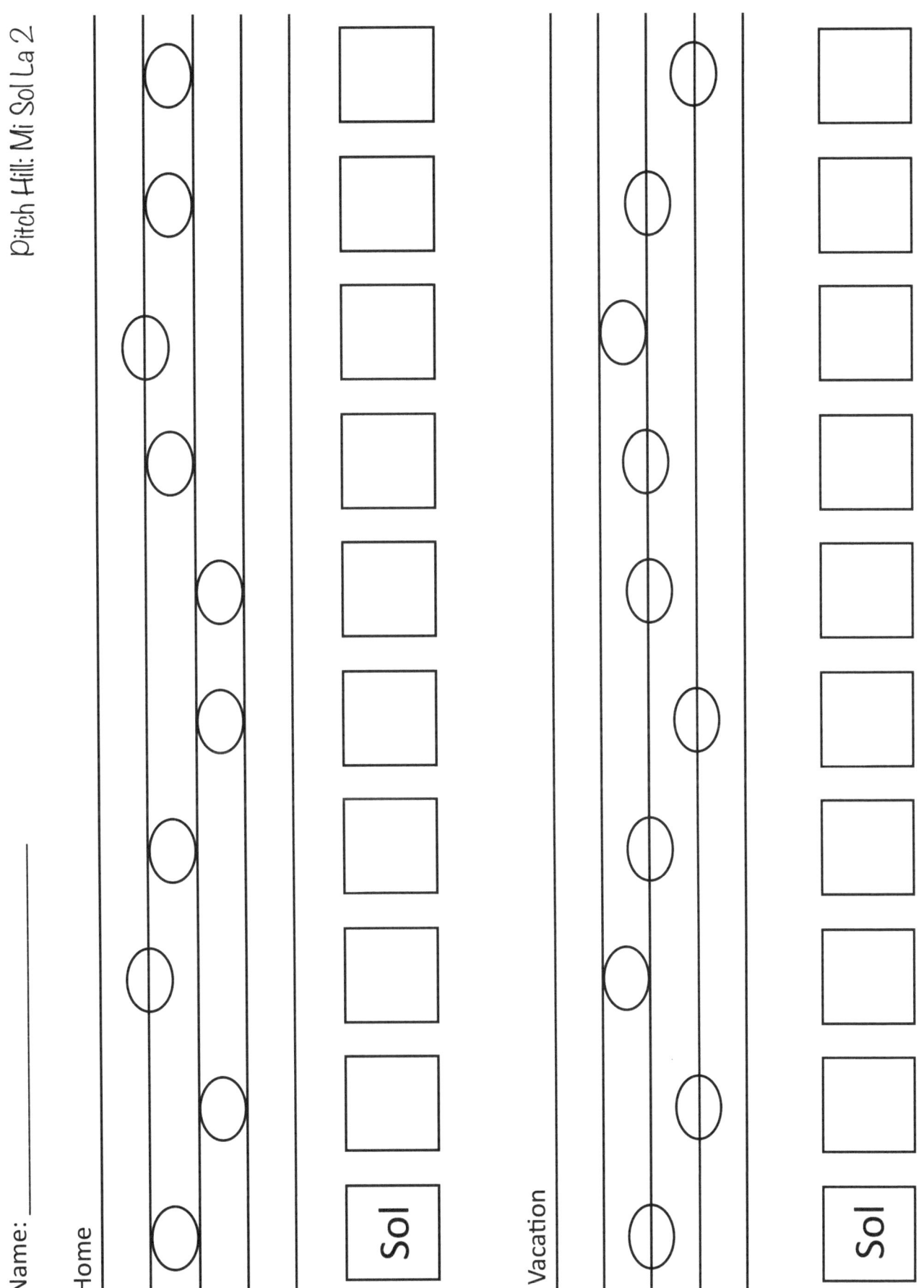

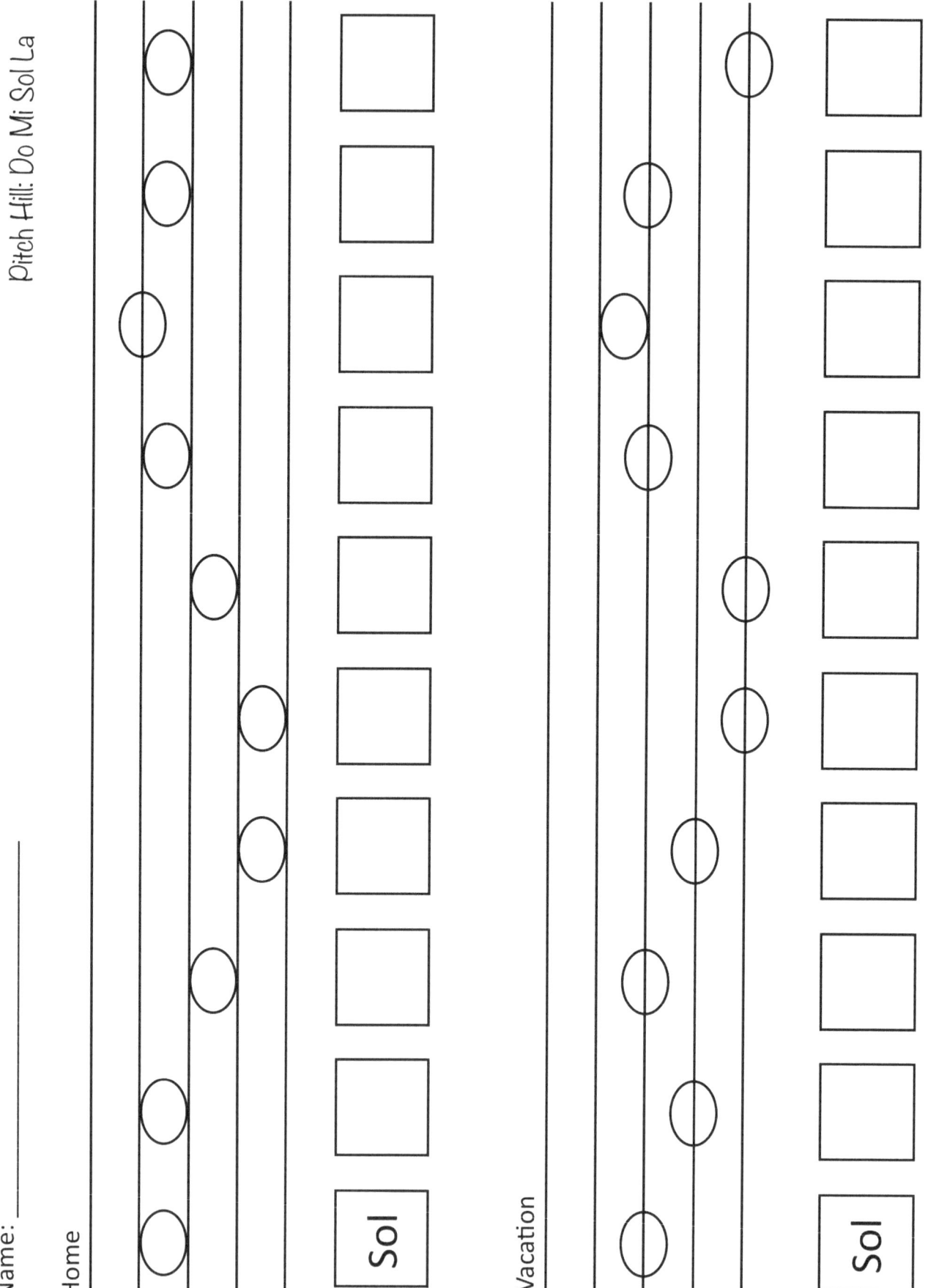

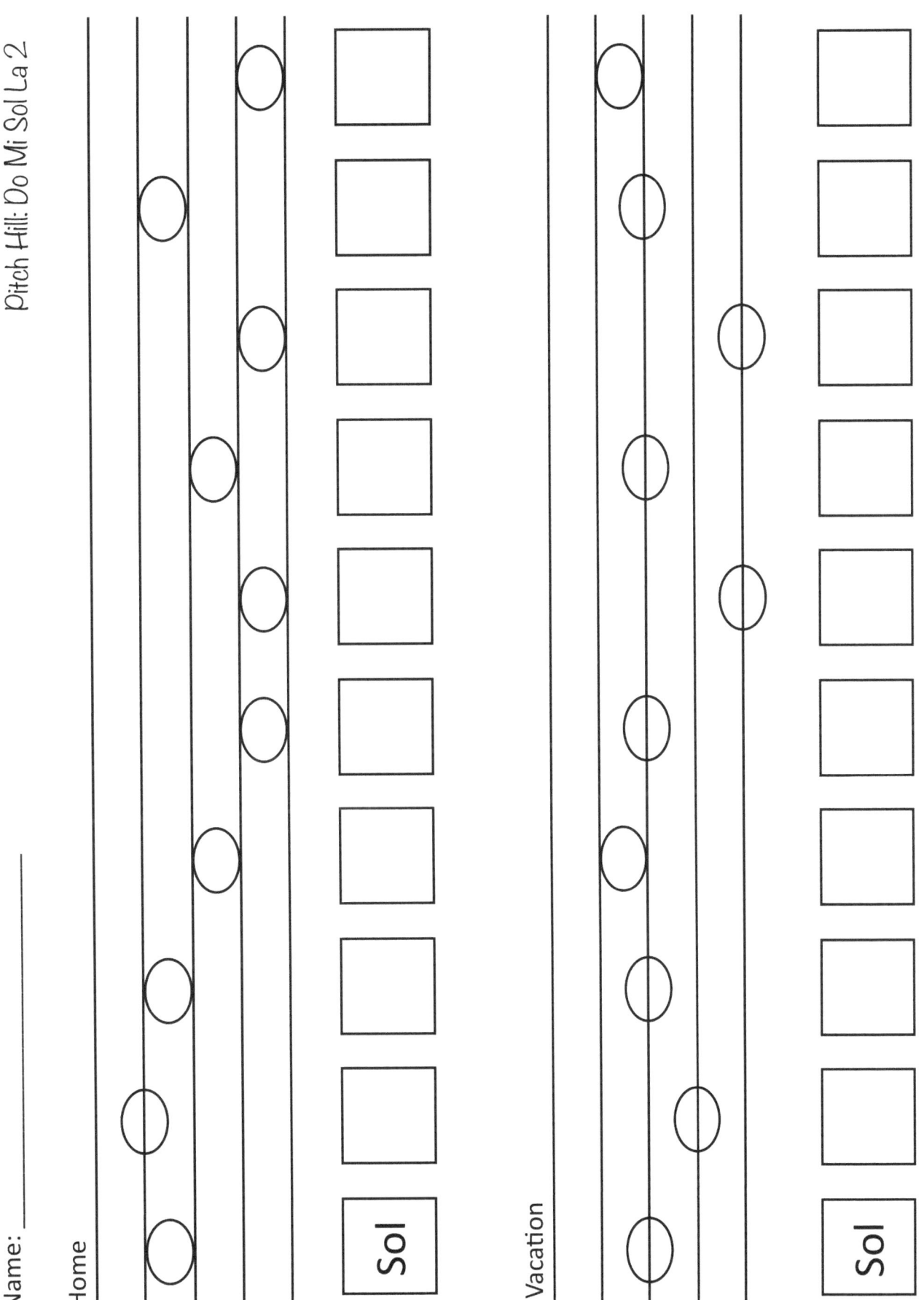

Name: _____

Pitch Hill: Do Re Mi Sol La

Home

Sol

Vacation

Sol

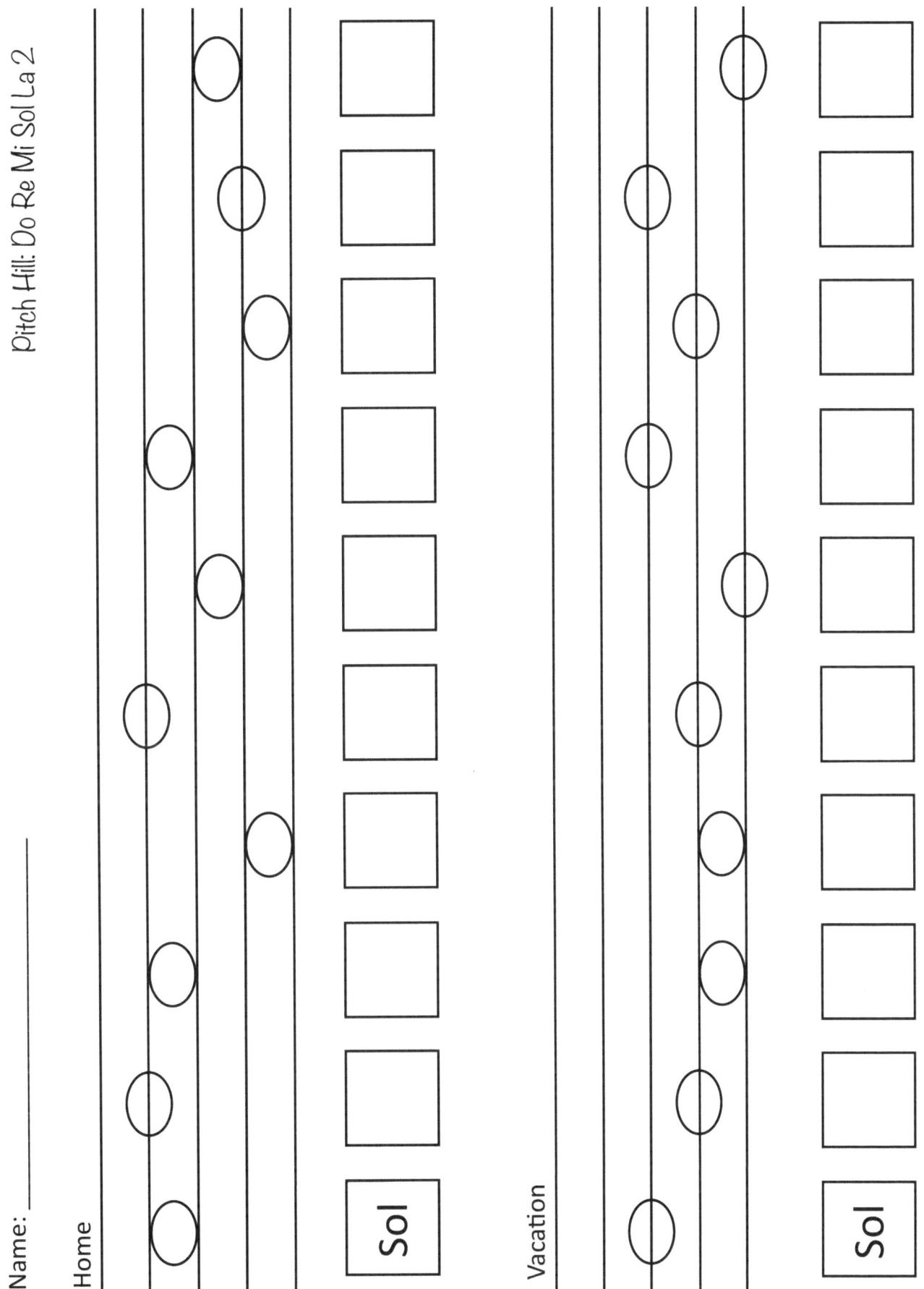

Name: _____

Pitch Hill: Do Re Mi Sol La
Mañana Iguana

Vacation

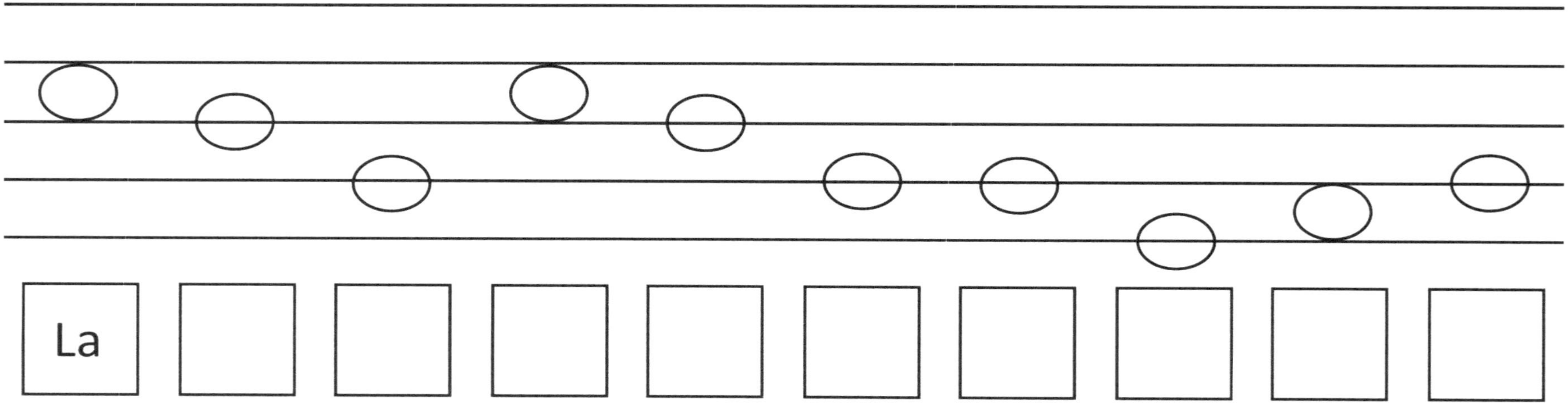

La "Mañ - an - a I - guan - a," is what they say!

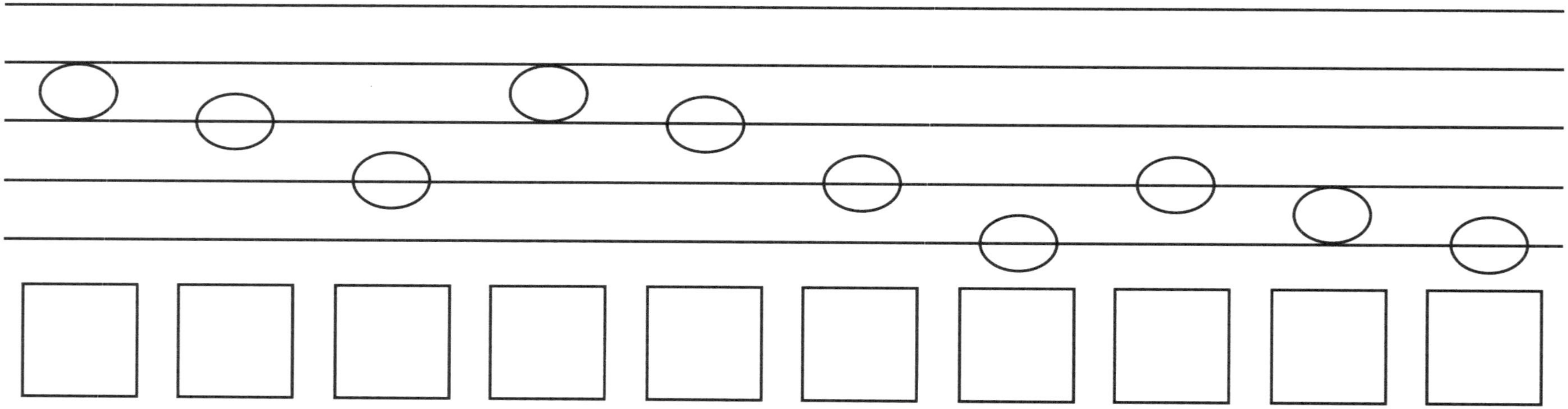

"Mañ - an - a I - guan - a," will be too late!

Name: _____

Pitch Hill: Do Re Mi

Home

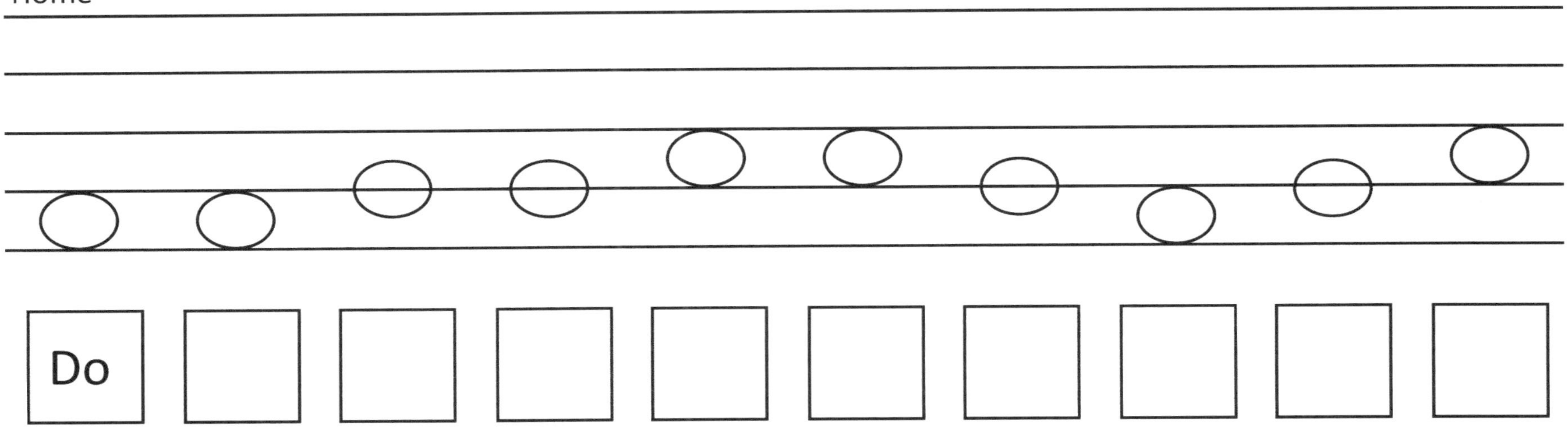

Do

Vacation

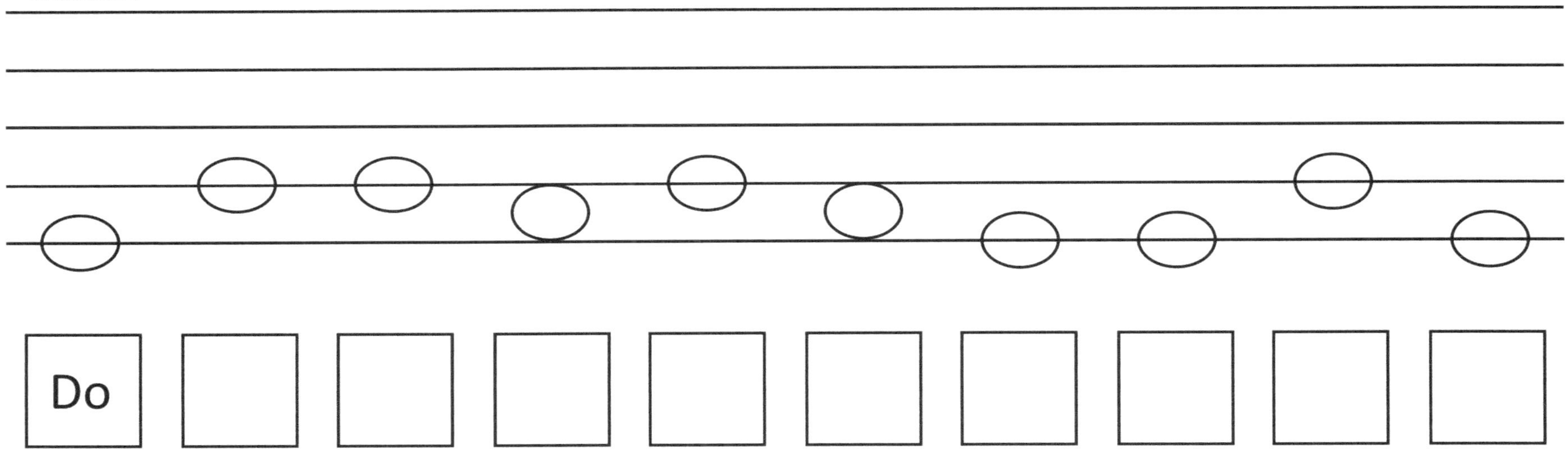

Do

Name: _____

Pitch Hill: Do Re Mi Fa
Silly Sally

Home

Do						
Sil	-	ly	Sal	-	ly	went	to	town,

Mi						
back	-	wards	up	-	side	down.

SHELLEY TOMICH

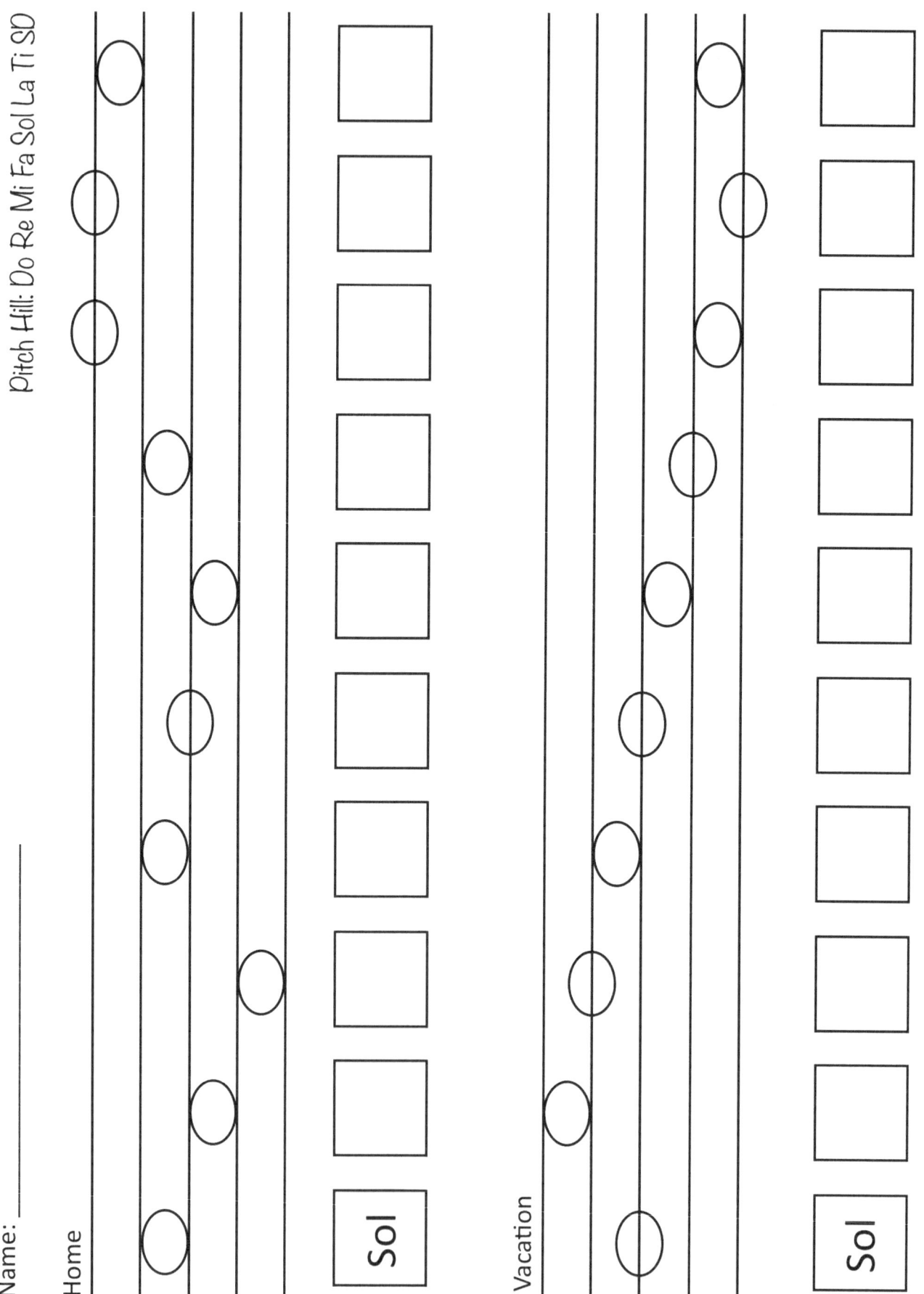

PITCH HILL

Name: _____   Pitch Hill: D R M F S L T SD Advanced

Home

Do							

Vacation

Do							

Home

Do							

Vacation

Do							

SHELLEY TOMICH

Pitch Hill: Blank Template

Name: _____

Name: _____ Pitch Hill: Blank Template Advanced

ACKNOWLEDGMENTS

Thank you to my friends and colleagues, Ginny Capps, Melissa Stouffer, Linda Seamons, Michelle Cygielman, Vanessa Edwards, and Kristina Whitley, who took the time to provide invaluable feedback on *Pitch Hill*; you are all brilliant teachers and wonderful people! Thank you to my husband, Mark, and my three daughters, Lucy, Evie, and Julie, for allowing me the time to finally write all this down!

I acknowledge with thanks the permission of the compilers, performers, and publishers mentioned below for the use of their copyrighted materials. Every effort has been made to trace the ownership of all copyrighted material and to secure the necessary permissions to reprint selections.

Boosey & Hawkes, Inc. for "'Round and 'Round" by Eleanor Locke. Copyright 1988 by Boosey & Hawkes, Inc. Used by permission of Boosey & Hawkes, Inc.

Rebecca Dennis for the use of the Curwen hand sign images. Used by permission of the artist.

Denise Fleming and Henry Holt and Co. for the use of the character "Cow" from *The Cow Who Clucked* by Denise Fleming. Used by permission of the publisher.

Jonathan London and Puffin for the use of the character "Froggy" and text from *Froggy Learns to Swim* by Jonathan London. Used by permission of the author.

North-South Books for the use of the character "Rainbow Fish" and images from *Rainbow Fish* by Marcus Pfister. Used by permission of the publisher.

Tiger Tales and Isobel Finn for the use of the character Ladybug from *The Very Lazy Ladybug* by Isobel Finn (ISBN: 978-1589255104) published by Tiger Tales. Used by permission of the publisher.

Sarah Oshea from Educlips for her beautiful illustrations. Used by permission of artist.

Charlie Tighe for the use of his composition, "Rainbow Fish." Used by permission of the composer.

Ann Whitford Paul and Holiday House for the use of the character "Iguana" and text from the book, *Manána Iguana* by Ann Whitford Paul. Used by permission of the publisher.

Audrey Wood for the text from *Ten Little Fish* and the character "Silly Sally" and text from *Silly Sally*, both by Audrey Wood. Used by permission of the author.

Michiko Yurko for the image "Curwen Hand Signs." Used and altered by permission of the artist.

Pearson Education for the song, "Pick a Pumpkin," from *The Magic of Music*. Copyright © 1965 Pearson Education, Inc. (Originally copyrighted by Ginn and Company). Used by permission. All Rights Reserved.

About the Author

Shelley Tomich is an elementary music specialist in Fulton County Schools (outside Atlanta, GA). She has experience teaching elementary band, chorus, and general music. She holds a Bachelors degree in Music Education-Instrumental from the University of Alabama, a Masters degree in Music Education-Choral/General Music from the University of Georgia, and the Educational Specialist degree in Technology in Schools from the University of Missouri. In addition she is Orff certified. Shelley lives in Atlanta with her husband and three daughters; when she is not teaching, she is reading or trying to grow things in the garden.

Want more fun with Pitch Hill?

Visit our website at

www.PitchHill.com

www.ingramcontent.com/pod-product-compliance
Lightning Source LLC
Chambersburg PA
CBHW041529220426
43671CB00002B/30